Business
as
Mission

Also by Dr. Kidane Araya:

Put God First

ISBN 978-1-77354-354-3 Paperback
978-1-77354-355-0 eBook
Also available in Tigrina and Amheric

Business
as
Mission

Dr. Kidane Araya

Published by Kidane Araya, Edmonton, Canada

ISBN 978-1-77354-352-9 Paperback
978-1-77354-352-9 eBook

Also available in Tigrina and Amheric

Publication assistance by

PAGEMASTER
PUBLISHING
PageMaster.ca

Acknowledgements

I wanted to express thanks to my counsellor and closest friend, Jesus Christ. He is the real author of this book and the finisher of my faith.

My heart, my faith, and my local church continue to lead me to talk about business as mission. I want to fulfill my calling of the great commission, as Jesus has instructed.

I would like to give thanks to my wife and family for the support they have shown me throughout my life. They have been with me through every endeavour and have encouraged me to accomplish anything I put my mind to.

Dr. Kidane Araya

June 10/2020

Preface

BUSINESS AS MISSION is a broad concept. There is a distinction between what people do and why they do it. The why is the topic that I want to expand on in this book.

The "business as mission" statement speaks about the reason people do what they do. It calls on believers to pursue the kingdom of God no matter where they are in their life journey. People can be found in all areas of life. They occupy different positions, places, domains, and in this vast world, people pursue life in many ways.

My hope in writing this book is to encourage people to engage in the world of business and to do so in a manner pleasing to God. Business can be done in a manner that is honest, faithful and right. Once we realize everything belongs to God, we begin to look at our responsibilities in that light. In this book, I will expand on how to work out this goal on a step-by-step basis and explain my reasoning further.

Dr. Kidane Araya

Contents

It is important

to honour God

in whatever it is

we do and keep

him in mind in

all that we do.

CHAPTER 01:

Trust in God to accomplish "Business as Mission"

BUSINESS AS MISSION! What does this mean exactly?

In my opinion, business as mission is a broad concept. God gives all an opportunity to make an impact in this world, through the people we meet, the community we engage with and nations we operate in. On the other hand, business as mission is a powerful way to expand the spiritual kingdom of God.

Business as mission plays out in many ways in the world. It changes based on current events, political, historical, and the economic environment. What is consistent is the framework of understanding the world. Wherever we are, we must serve the kingdom of God. That begins by firstly putting your trust in God.

When something happens unexpectedly in our life, a certain gap is created, and we can't see how to surpass it, overcome it, or move through it. At these times, we must stay close to God and accept His words. He said all is good for those who love him and dedicate his life to him. In these situations, we must trust God wholeheartedly and offer prayers.

Whenever you come across something insurmountable in your life, such as an economic disaster, the loss of family members, the problem of having not being able to have children, a severe illness, or any of these terrible things that can happen, ask God to come into your situation.

Can your brain even imagine or think about it? Continue to pray. No matter how hopeless it may seem, do not stop thanking God. When you love him and trust him for your future, he will do things in your life.

Today, I am talking to you about your trust in God. You believe in God. When you trust in God, God blesses you and unites with you. You do not have to fear because you trust God. He is faithful and strong enough to break every chain in your life. He can sustain you.

You have always trusted Him, and you will continue to trust Him forever. He is proud of you. He has seen your trust and your faith, and He will return it to you.

You believe in the Lord, that's good. You do not have to fear, because God is with you. Believing in God means that you have complete faith in God and you are a very strong person. In all the things you've experienced in your life, even if you have doubts and challenges, you must still believe God is faithful.

Pray to him, saying, "Lord, I believe in you, I believe in what you say. At every stage of my life, I will believe in you. Every day, you are loyal." This is your belief and your voice, so God will lead you through the difficulties. Your best day is coming because you believe in Jesus Christ. Isn't it incredible?

We live in a world where everyone will disappoint you at some point; even the best people or the most supportive ones will let you down. It doesn't even matter if you were very close to them. Everyone will disappoint you from time to time because no one is perfect.

God will never disappoint you. He just needs time, and his timing is often unpleasant, of course. This is what I am saying here. God's timing is unimaginable. Therefore, you have faith in God.

You are a trusted person, and you have trusted God because he is reliable.

Reasons to trust God

He is absolute

There is not even a single percent chance that God's word is not complete and absolute truth. The announcements He makes are not ninety percent true or ninety-nine percent, they are one hundred percent true. If even one finding was not accurate, we could not believe him completely. If even one percent were not true, we wouldn't know which part to accept as truth.

As a trusting Christian, I ultimately believe that God will settle everything, and this phrase helps me every time I pass through challenging times. Knowing I could completely trust his terms has given me hope I had never known. We trust in God as his word is true.

He doesn't lie

Human beings lie. Unfortunately, even Christians sometimes lie. But God is infinitely holy. He only speaks the truth. As we all know, Satan will try to make us question the authenticity of God. So, the question is always, what do I believe — my eyes, my feelings, my assessment of things, or God's word? God has never lied. So we can trust the authenticity of God.

He never changes

Human beings constantly change. From babies to children, from teenagers to adults, our bodies change. Over the years, our tastes and preferences continuously change. Many years ago, I loved iced tea, and I used to drink a lot. Now I don't care for it.

But God will never change his existence. Today, he is the same as he was and will remain like this forever. We can believe in God because God will never change.

He never changes his mind

God will never change, and He will never change His mind. He didn't say, "Well, I know I said people should respect their parents, but the world has changed. People no longer have to do that." No, God never changes his mind; and as he never changes his mind, we can trust him.

He sticks to his plans

God doesn't start with a plan for the world, then amend it if things don't go perfectly. He has set purposes for each of us, which he will certainly fulfil. The purpose he has set for you will be fulfilled, no matter how many times we have failed. The plans of God are not dependent on the actions of human beings. Considering the fact, he sticks to his plans, we must trust him in all situations.

He has always fulfilled his words

God fulfilled every promise he made to the Israelites. He took them out of the promised land of slavery. He humbled all their enemies. None of his good promises failed.

I have seen that God has fulfilled many good promises in my life. I still want him to keep his promises. Even if I have not seen them in my life, I know that I will be in heaven seeing how he fulfills all that he promised. Because he has always fulfilled his promises, we can believe in God.

He is sovereign over all things

We can make a promise, and then a change in the situation can stop us from fulfilling that promise. I may agree to pick you up at 1:00 and then be demoralized on my way to your house. Other things come up that stop us from fulfilling our promises.

But nothing can stop God. He has sovereignty over every molecule in the universe. He has dominion over all angels and all demons. Satan and all his servants cannot stop God from saving people, providing us with food, and fulfilling his plan for us.

He is wise

If God did not have infinite wisdom, it would be a terrible world. But because he is wise, he knows the best way in every situation. Because he is infinitely wise, his promise is perfect. Because of his infinite wisdom, everything he said is true, perfect, and the best for us. So, we can trust him.

He is completely just

If I have to appear before a judge with a reputation for being unfair, I will be scared. But God is infinite and totally righteous. He always does the right thing. He will never do anything unjust. He has never done anything wrong. So, we can trust him.

He has wonderful plans

How reliable is our God? He has many gifts of grace in store for us; he is waiting to give them to us. He has a good plan for us, and nothing can stop him from achieving, proving we can trust Him.

As entrepreneurs, we are always in an uncertain state. The product we launch may not be a hit, large customers may leave us, employees may steal something from us, or lawsuits may fall on us. All of these things could happen to us in our company, or we see this possibility elsewhere. But as a godly entrepreneur, I should still look to God and believe he has planned all my many twists and turns.

It is not easy for us to believe in God forever, especially when the bank account is close to zero and precisely when we are not sure how to pay the salaries on the 15th.

Trust is a fragile thing, and given past pains and experiences, trust is extremely difficult for most people. We have been burned by lies, disappointments from people, or the environment. We trust people in our business and get betrayed. We pin our hopes on a particular product, service or marketing activity, but it ultimately fails. The size of the company is irrelevant; I have seen many entrepreneurs who doubt.

Trust is one of the most crucial pillars of Christian entrepreneurship. Believe that God is leading us through the process, and believe that, whatever the outcome, God is our master, who is the key to the success of our business. But for many of us, our experience makes us feel scared, insecure, and unable to act.

In the Bible:

> "Trust in the Lord with all your heart; do not depend on your own understanding. Seek his will in all you do, and he will show you which path to take. Don't be impressed with your own wisdom. Instead, fear the Lord and turn away from evil. Then you will have healing for your body and strength for your bones." – Proverbs 3:5-8 NLT

This proverb enlightens why you need to trust God. God is like the chairman of your company's board of directors. You are the "president" of the company; He is the Chief Executive Officer. In this posture, you admit he is strong, intense and perfect. Close your eyes and imagine walking into his office in the morning and believe that no matter what happens, his plan is constantly under review. It will benefit you to view the plan.

When you can accept it as your business plan and process, you will move in the right direction to achieve important things, and that direction will move towards what you are born to do.

As Christian business people, we put God before the word entrepreneur and approach him because we recognize he has a direct interest in our business direction. I know it is difficult for us to believe what we do not see or to make a return on investment, but we must use the power of trust in God.

When we do not trust God in our daily business life, we take control away from God about future situations and leave everything to the market to determine our destiny. The market does not want you to exist. God is a worthy guide, and this world is a bad place.

Today, take a moment to imagine God as the CEO and you as the President. Even if you don't fully understand the plan for you, trust him. Wait and see if God will do more than you think. Regardless of the waiting time or circumstances, believe in God's procedures.

This is a business; we don't understand or know what will happen! As Christians, we must have faith in God. This is not something we have done once. This is a daily thing. We must constantly realize that God has a plan for our business in the marketplace. God is 100% in control, even if it appears he is not there. Let us believe in the authenticity and reliability of God.

Therefore, it is time for us to trust God in everything and stop running our businesses by relying on our own wisdom, understanding and human knowledge, for he has perfect and absolute wisdom and knowledge of everything.

Trusting in God is your business. You need to rely on the integrity and reliability of God to guide you through important life decisions and protect you from catastrophic errors. So, when things are bad for you, who are you looking at?

I know there are many people who are successful in business but have nothing to do with God, but when their wealth is a tragedy, look at their morals and attitudes. Their trust lies in their business and their finances. Money is their God, so their faith is as fragile and changeable as the things they trust.

As Christians, we must ensure our trust is solely the property of the eternal God.

CHAPTER 02:

Christian business principles

BUSINESS LEADERS OFTEN want to know where to find the best business advice and tips to build their own business. While many books have been written by excellent business consultants, business leaders only need to know one book that contains all the best business secrets to building a successful business and life.

That holy book is the Bible. I have studied the Bible for many years and often read words that encourage, comfort, heal and inspire. I have also found it contains the best principles for building a successful business. The following principles will help any leader expand their business and influence so they can hear the word "well done" in this and their next life.

As Christian business owners, entrepreneurs and professionals, God calls us to conduct our business with morality and ethics. We have been delegated the world's resources, and we need to manage them carefully and skillfully. We have a responsibility to honour God by observing and following God's principles.

Many of us have held various positions in the workforce. Some have even left careers to seek the profession that God has placed in their hearts. During my entrepreneurial journey, I observed the following Christian business principles:

Belief in God

"Trust in the Lord with all your heart; do not depend on your own understanding." (Proverbs 3:5 NLT)

God wants us to believe in everything. It does not just mean we believe in his personal life, but we need to include our professional experience as well. As Christian business experts, we rely on the Lord's leadership and governance in the business world. We need to pursue God's blessings and grace for our work. When we plead and trust him to provide strategic direction, resources and funding, we have the confidence to take action. When we choose faith, it has the ability to open the door and create more opportunities.

Attentiveness

"Never be lazy, but work hard and serve the Lord enthusiastically." - Romans 12:11 NLT.

All the great men of the Bible are workers, and many people work even when God calls them. God is busy, not lazy. God wants us to be productive, whatever his size, to use our knowledge, talents and capacities. Hard work is essential for doing business, showing God that we are grateful for His resources, and we do not intend to waste them. If we faithfully use what God has given us in every season of life, we can glorify God at any professional and business level.

Honesty

"The Lord is more pleased when we do what is right and just than when we offer him sacrifices." - Proverbs 21:3 NLT

God is righteous, so we must conduct business with honesty and integrity. Fair treatment is not only a biblical principle but can also improve business relationships with employees, colleagues and customers. What is important is that we must strictly fulfil our promises, be honest, do only good and acceptable work of the Lord, and avoid actions that may be beneficial but morally wrong.

Big-heartedness

Each of you should use whatever gift you have received to help others as faithful stewards of God's grace in its various forms.

The Lord is generous, kind, and compassionate. A Godly company will use these qualities and strive to go beyond self-sufficiency; they help others. Christian business professionals go beyond worldly generosity and support people in society because God so blesses us. Charity becomes an internal motivation, giving the Holy Spirit the way and the position to guide us. For those who don't understand, this can seem dangerous or naïve, but Christian business professionals believe that God's rewards outweigh earthly rewards.

We are born with unique abilities and talents, which are very important to our profession and career. Allowing God to mature and use these abilities will enable him to increase and strengthen us in a greater measure than we could possibly achieve alone. Use your gifts and talents wisely and stand out in your profession. Regardless of what career we are involved in, we all should honour God.

Going the extra-mile

Go a little further. Always do something more than expected and anticipated. Try to surprise others by giving consideration to minor things that other individuals ignore, and be different.

The principle of going the extra mile helps build life and conduct in business. Good companies will develop an extra mile mentality.

Jesus himself gave this principle in Matthew. "If a soldier demands that you carry his gear for a mile, carry it two miles." – Matthew 5:41 NLT.

Jesus gave his followers this principle as a way of separating them from their own culture. A way to help others see it more clearly. In business, we also need to distinguish ourselves so others can see our business clearly. Too many companies expect an extra mile result without paying an extra mile effort. It's always a good idea to go farther than expected. Every company is wise to cultivate the extra mile of thinking throughout the whole business.

However, many companies expect you to go the extra mile without the intention of rewarding you for that mile.

Thoughtfulness

Put individuals first and then make things. Treat your teams like you want to be treated. This can be achieved by practising thoughtfulness. When you care for the customers and the employees, they will certainly think of you.

Luke 6:31 sets out useful biblical principles for building a business. This verse is known as the Golden Rule, and states that we should "do things for others as you want others to do for you." Many great companies are based on this principle. Following the Golden Rule has helped develop my business and see it thrive into a successful company. Someone once told me: "I don't remember a time when my rule was not the golden rule, but the torch that shaped my footprint." This concept is to think of others first. Prudent business leaders and companies will treat others as they wish to be treated.

Companies that don't look after their clients will not be looked after by their clients.

Find purpose with the profit

Know your priorities. Live and run your business with goals and vision. Profits are strong. Maximizing profit can bring success and meaning to the business. Attract others to carry out your mission and dream. Always explain your reasons.

Every successful business generates profit. It is often mentioned in business circles that you only have a business if you make a profit. Every company aims to be profitable, however; Christian leaders know wrong profits can cause havoc.

The biblical principle Christian leaders must follow is to build a purposeful and profitable business. Jesus questioned his followers, "and what do you benefit if you gain the whole world but lose your own soul?" - Mark 8:36 NLT. This verse teaches the power that every Christian leader should follow the Principle.

Profit is undoubtedly good, but profit used for doing good is even better.

Identifying when to say Yes or No

Analyze and make an informed decision. Make value-based decisions. Know when to say "no." Say "yes" to things that can make you and your organization better. Live up to your words. Make your signature carry meaning, and always keep your promises.

The ability to make a quick decision is the key to persuasive leadership. People cannot follow individuals who do not identify where they are heading or why they are moving in the direction they are going. Christ gives a secret to leaders in Matthew where he says, "Do not even say, 'By my head!' for you can't turn one hair white or black. Just say a simple, 'Yes, I will,' or 'No, I won't.' Anything beyond this is from the evil one." – Matthew 5:36-37 NLT.

The control to say "yes" or "no" quickly means you know the direction you want to go and the tasks you want to do. Make your words meaningful. By communicating with others, they can rely on you and your commitment to developing and building trust. Many leaders drop their influence with others because of their lack of commitment to ideals. Leaders must know their "no" and say "yes" or "no" quickly.

Identify your No's because your "no's" make all the difference in business.

Make the move that reflects steward leadership

Practice steward leadership in your daily routine. Make sure to use resources intelligently. Recollect that God owns it all, and he will reward that individual who uses his resources to their maximum proficiency. Be prepared to answer for all of your decisions. Prepare yourself to hear the words "well done."

A significant shift for Christian business owners is steering from ownership to stewardship. Jesus Christ told a story in Matthew about a faithful servant. He finished the story with the words: "The master said, 'Well done, my good and faithful servant. You have been faithful in handling this small amount, so now I will give you many more responsibilities. Let's celebrate together!'" – Mathew 25:23 NLT.

Well Done, these two words are very influential in the English language. It must be the desire of every Christian business owner to hear these words at the end of their journey.

Well done is the greatest reward; we Christians must work hard to hear this from God in the end.

Have faith in the law of sowing and reaping

Sow bountifully. Be substantial with the seeds you are planting daily. Make yourself open to trying new things. Don't be afraid to start a small business. You can see it grow with the help of practice and patience.

Laws of life are fundamental and can be trusted, as they have stood the test of time. Successful businesses distinguish and trust the laws of sowing and reaping. In the book of 2 Corinthians, the Bible says, "Remember this—a farmer who plants only a few seeds will get a small crop. But the one who plants generously will get a generous crop" – 2 Corinthians 9:6 NLT.

A modern translation of the Bible understands this principle with these words. "Remember that a farmer who plants only a few seeds will get a lesser crop. But the one who plants bigheartedly will get a generous crop."

Don't be afraid to start with a small amount of seed. The yield you are reaping today is from the seeds that you planted yesterday.

Also, another part of the Bible reminds the readers that we will reap what we sow. For that reason, so sow generously and be on a constant lookout to reap your yield.

The crop you are reaping today is from the seeds you planted yesterday.

Believe and request for the impossible

Dream big and impossible dreams. Set big unworldly goals. Stretch yourself and push yourself to the maximum. Find better ways to look at old problems—grip belief. Pray big prayers and expect unbelievable answers.

Everything starts with a big dream. The world is healthier when individuals dream big and believe that impossible things can also happen. Challenge yourself to request "what if" questions and use your imagination to see the world in fresh and better ways. The individuals wish to be with leaders and organizations who have immense visions.

Ephesians 3:20,21 says, "Now to him who is able to do infinitely more than all we ask or visualize, as per his power that is at work within us, to him be glory in the church and Jesus Christ throughout all generations, forever and ever! Amen." God wants to pursue things that excite you. Dream bigger and request God to do more than you ask or dream. A big vision motivates and attracts. Supersize your thoughts and your beliefs.

Whatever seems impossible to man is possible for God.

Build something that lasts for a long time

Work on the more significant projects. Always do something big. Distinguish your essential values and beliefs and be a forward thinker. Make decisions with tomorrow in mind. Get yourself ready for the future by making the perfect decision today. Distinguish your foundation.

Don't waste time building a test that won't last. Building on the factual foundation will help your business withstand the storm of market changes. The key to building a successful business is to act honestly in any situation. Integrity means doing the right thing at all times under any circumstances.

Martin Luther King Jr. learned: "It's always right to do the right thing." He may have taken inspiration from the Bible in Proverbs 4: 25. The Bible Says, "Look your eyes straight ahead; fix your gaze directly before you. Think carefully about your steps and stay firm. Do your best. Don't turn right or left; keep your feet away from evil." Build on a solid foundation. Business is built on the previous reputation. Companies without a solid foundation are on slippery ground that can collapse at any time.

Our destiny beckons in the future, but it is molded by the decisions that we make today.

Understand the order of things and work the directive

Strive for clarity. Seek first the ideologies of God and his kingdom. Distinguish your priorities. Rehearse the art of first fruits in all aspects of life and leadership.

The correct order is essential. When leaders understand the order of things, everything flows so much better. Jesus gave followers a vital principle in Matthew 6:33. Jesus said, "But first seek his kingdom and righteousness, and all these things shall be given to you."

The first three words of the verse are informative. These words are "but seek first". An essential principle in business practice is to focus on the first thing. Leaders must understand the order of things. Leaders must remain alert and be transparent in everything. Put God and his principles first. Believe his commandments, seek his kingdom first.

When a leader appreciates the order of things, things become easier to apprehend.

Improving the team means improving the organization

Find the right and honest individuals to bring around you.

Make God's creation your top priority. There is always something to learn from people. Spend time with a wise squad of mentors. Learn faster by wisdom from others. Ask questions and listen. Seek advice and help people to discover their gifts and capacities. Find reliable and passionate people.

Great leaders can absorb from others, and they learn at a much faster pace. You need a team around you to inspire and help you build something more important than what you could build on your own.

No great leader has accomplished something significant on their own. So, to become one, you must find your desire and add passionate people to your team. Enthusiasts perform better. Ephesians 2:10 states: "You are the work of God, created to do the good works that God has prepared in advance." The power of this principle is profound and incredible.

This verse reminds Christian business leaders that their founding is purposeful. In fact, not only are they purposeful, everyone in the team serves a purpose. When the company discovers employees' talents and passions, and finds out how to release those passions, individuals and companies will enjoy higher productivity.

Passionate people are trustworthy people. The wisdom of others can be powerful. Every great leader in the Bible has at least one counsellor. However, many business leaders try to do everything themselves. It is said that it is lonely at the top. If you want to lead alone, it will be lonely. But real leaders believe in the power of others.

When your people get better, your organization becomes better.

Do things today that will make an impact

Invest intelligently. Don't forget to spend on yourself. Make the right reserves to help the business to grow. Invest in your individuals. Invest and grow your commitment and your desire.

A principle that has molded many trades and business leaders is Matthew 6:21; "Where your wealth is, there is where your heart will be."

Investment is another word for treasure. Front-runners are called to lead with all of their heart. Therefore, a leader should make investments cleverly. A leader must make use of the funds of the company to make the correct investments in the business, individuals, and infrastructure. When businesses are invested in sensibly, the business will grow. Worthy investments set the direction and the track of a business to ensure its growth and development. When an enterprise is abandoned, it will shrink and eventually die.

With careful and intelligent investment the business will grow.

Work to make things perfect

Excellent work is worth it. Make every effort to achieve more meaningful goals and higher careers. Continually improve and strive to improve products and services. Demonstrate your value through high-quality products.

Building a business based on biblical principles requires changing perspectives. For Christian leaders, a fundamental approach is to practice excellence at all times and under all circumstances. The apostle Paul transcribed these critical words in Colossians 3: 23,24. He said: "No matter what you do, you must work wholeheartedly for God, not for the master of humanity, because you know you will receive an inheritance from God as a reward."

Paul reminds Christian leaders that their lives are a higher calling. Christians are required to do all work with distinction. When you pursue excellence in everything, you listen to the "accomplishments" of employees, customers, and God.

Excellent work is everlasting work.

CHAPTER 03:

Understand the Christian business concept

WHY DO WE, as Christians, need God in business?

Christians must understand the concept of business in Christianity. There are two different statements of purpose. One is an internal observation; the other is an external comment. Externally, business is the only organization that creates economic value. Universities provide intellectual capital but do not create things. Business accepts these ideas and commercializes them. Business plays a crucial role in creating products and services.

However, in God's eyes, not all products an enterprise can produce are equally good. Therefore, the Christian in business not only asks what will create profit but also asks what kind of products or services should be produced, taking into account the core capabilities and assets under his control which could best serve his community.

As Christian business owners, it can be complicated to navigate the best way to operate your business in honour of Jesus Christ. Doing business the way God wants it requires well-planned strategies for everything from hiring excellent staff to managing your finances in a way that respects God.

The general concept for Christian businesses

Christian businesses should be dedicated to more than the profit motive. Adding value, enhancing the quality of life, and improving society – these are the ways in which businesses can glorify Jesus.

Acting with truthfulness, credibility, and morality in your day-to-day processes is imperative. Integrity in the Christian sense perhaps means you act as to what you say you are.

The concepts of business in Christianity can be represented by fair prices, excellent customer service, fair treatment of employees, and honest advertising. As noted in Colossians 3:23, "whatever you do, work heartily, as for the Lord and not for men."

Putting in great efforts reflects the Christian spirit. Proverbs 22:29 suggests that we should work diligently and skillfully.

The overall excellence of your products and services reflects what is said in Titus 3:8 "...those who have trusted in God may be careful to devote themselves to doing what is good. These things are excellent and profitable for everyone."

Review all your procedures and policies and make sure they comply with these essential Christian principles.

Studies have shown that Christian companies can encourage employees to reduce fear and increase investment. From operations to long-term strategies, applying these general principles in everything can help you praise God more efficiently in your daily work. The result can be a more prosperous and meaningful workplace for you and your employees.

Hiring right and commitment to team-members

Finding employees with similar interests and beliefs is essential. Find employees who are dedicated to quality and excellence,

and who have the perfect skills to deliver the high standards expected from your organization.

After hiring employees correctly, you need to show your employees' commitment (Colossians 4: 1). Giving employees fair com-
pensation, training, and growth opportunities. Provide feedback to
employees for improvement and advancement. Communicate with
employees who serve Jesus at work (Colossians 3: 22-24). It is also
significant to make sure your default super fund is an ethical fund
like Christian Super.

Be an example as a leader by being the best and performing
the best. As Matthew 10:25 says, "It is adequate for students to be
like the teachers, and servants like the masters."

Managing finances

When it comes to managing finances as a Christian business,
it's helpful to recall numerous passages from the Bible.

"The rich rule over the one who is poor, and the borrower
becomes the slave to the lender." (Proverbs 22:7) "But love your
opponents, do good to them, and lend to them without expecting
anything in return. Then your reward will be unlimited, and you
will be offspring of the Highest because he is kind to the unthank-
ful and wicked." (Luke 6.35)

The first paragraph suggests that unless you are willing to
burden your future, you should not borrow money to finance your
business. The second paragraph can be interpreted as a good loan,
but only if you treat it as a gift.

Christian ethics suggest you should manage your business
assets diligently and act according to moral concepts such as honesty, purity and fair pricing. Make sure your company's financial
records are comprehensive, transparent, and manage funds respon-
sibly.

Dealing with challenging situations

Problematic situations are part of any business. These situations include challenges in finances, integrity and resource limitations, as well as the loyalty of the customer to your trademark.

Integrity

Maintaining integrity is a daily challenge. Avoid cutting corners and make sure you are transparent in understanding the issues your customers should be aware of. When you compromise integrity, it is possible to damage customer trust. Let your organization and your team find ethical solutions to everyday challenges.

Financial management

Focus on managing cash flow and avoid spending that exceeds your capabilities. Avoid borrowing money to do business. If you need more capital to expand, look for alternatives like equity. Seek financial advice on corporate asset management.

Loyalty to your brand

Competition can make maintaining brand loyalty a challenge. Look for cost-effective networks, such as social media, to improve customer contact. Explore innovative ways to maintain customer engagement and interest.

Compliance and regulation

Christian principles of diligence and integrity imply that you need to ensure your organization reflects high standards of compliance. In many industries, regulations are continuously changing, so must accept and adapt the right internal changes. Maintaining compliance is essential not only for the integrity of the law and risk management but also for your corporate reputation.

Keeping God at the front position of your organization

As a Christian business owner, you will want to conduct business in accordance with the high-level principles you follow in your private life. Honesty and fairness are general principles that are essential for everyday work. Treating your staff legally and avoiding loans are also important concepts of Christian organizations.

Through loyalty to Christian ideals and teachings, your work will honour God as the principle of a true Christian's cause.

The facets of a Christian business

1. God owns the earth and everything present in it.

This comprises all animals, all plants, and even all businesses. In my opinion, the first step to a Christian business is to recognize this fact and submit the leadership of the business to God's direction. Only God is in charge of everything, and only he has the power to control everything.

2. God's economy functions from an eternal perspective.

God's economy is not based on 30 days (nor quarterly or yearly). Therefore, Christian companies conduct business from an eternal point of view - this choice has an everlasting impact on financial performance. Obviously, there is no business if you ignore financial performance, but you can achieve both short and long-term rewards as long as you follow God's principles.

3. Christian business does not guarantee wealth.

While TV preachers tell you other things, dedicating your business to God does not guarantee your financial success. Although God promised that if we dedicate our efforts to Him, He will honour our efforts (Psalm 37: 5-6) but he did not say when it will happen. It's his schedule is not ours. When we respect him, we might expect to be rewarded, but we may not achieve it for 100 years. We honour him for his identity, not for what he brings.

4. The mission of the Christian business matches with Scripture.

The Utmost Commandment (Matt. 22:37-40) "Jesus said to him, you shall love the Lord your God with all your heart, and with all your soul, and with all your mind," are instructions, not suggestions. Therefore, I believe the Christian business should have a mission that reflects these instructions.

5. A Christian business exists and functions in the "world."

It employs believers and non-believers alike. It is a platform for believers as well as clients and the community in the ordinary course of doing business. This organization takes on a variety of looks!

6. A Christian business will be sufficient for us.

In short, we are designed to have everything we need through our relationship with God. If we try to separate our work from that relationship, hoping we can achieve different material achievements, then we are sad. For more information, read about the missionaries. On the other hand, even the humble job, if given to God, will bring us incredible achievements.

7. Becoming a Christian business leader.

One of the vital characteristics of a Christian business leader is modesty. The example of Jesus Christ washing the feet of his followers continues to be the most prominent reminder of this.

As Henri Nouwen said, "The path of the Christian leader is not the way of upward flexibility in which our world has invested so much, but the way of downward movement ending on the cross."

The Gospel tells of the night before Jesus finally fulfilled his goal - to be arrested, crucified, and then to resurrect, to free us from sin. He was not about to make a prestigious speech. Instead, he bent down. When he washed their dirty feet with his own hands and told them to do the same; he led them from the lowest position. (John 13: 1-17)

Jesus' example is in stark contrast to our modern culture. Leaders are supposed to arrogant. They are to stand tall. But Jesus tells us something different. He is bigger and more magnificent than his competitors. As an entrepreneur who strives to be like Jesus when you start, grow and lead a successful career, how will you lead like him? How do the examples of foot washing reflect on how you operate in a business environment? These are the questions you need to find answers for by yourself. One can only find answers to all such questions by following the path of Jesus.

8. Communicating your vision.

Any successful business needs an efficient communicator to show the market why the business offerings have value and to whom. Many even use a word borrowed from religion – evangelism – to describe this.

Dr. Martin Luther King Jr. understood that there are two types of laws in this world, those that are made by a superior authority and those that are made by ordinary men. … We followed him – not for him, but for the better version of ourselves. He communicated vision.

Paul communicated vision in Acts when he said: "So you do not know what you worship. 'This is what I'm announcing to you.'" (Acts 17:23) Then he showed them the true God of the Bible.

The entrepreneur must understand what the vision is, and that it is important and how to value others. The Bible will help you visualize your vision based it's values. At the same time, it will also provide some excellent examples of spreading the Gospel.

9. Serving with integrity.

The Bible advises individuals to serve God and others happily and do what you say you're going to do authentically. This is another vital part of being a fruitful entrepreneur.

Jesus made this clear. The legal expert asked him which is the largest order. He said: "Love the Lord your God with all your heart, with all your soul, and with all your mind." This is the first and greatest order. The second one is this: "Love your neighbour as much as you love yourself" (Matthew 22: 37-39)

When Christian leaders cannot lead in an upright manner, it is almost always because they have not followed these two commandments. The biblical foundation as an entrepreneur will help you remember the power of seeking God's wisdom and fulfilling your promises.

10. Performing Christian ethics.

Ethics is the study of goodness most often applied to business: The ethics of the Christian ground your business viewpoint and actions in biblical philosophies.

To be a Christian businessman means to forgive the unforgivable, as God has forgiven the inexcusable in you. The Bible is beneficial for a Christian entrepreneur's decision-making, especially when it comes to problems such as:

» Making appointment and dismissal decisions as the business grows.
» Dealing with clients who fail to make payments timely.
» Negotiating with salespersons who supply your business with services and goods.

When dealing with money and personnel issues, it is easy to make emotional decisions. In these situations, Jesus' parables often suggest finding a way to provide forgiveness. One of them is that the servant after the owner has forgiven his servant's debt, will ask the debtor to repay all debts. When the owner finds out, he will be furious, just as God will be with us. (Matthew 18: 21-35)

But, is it best to let go, or do you take legal action for granted? Yes. The critical thing you will learn in the Christian Moral Plan is to seek the words of the heart and God when making these difficult decisions.

11. Consider the entrepreneurial soul and the Holy Spirit.

Finally, considering how your drive and the Holy Spirit may or may not be leading in you the same way is also essential. Being a Christian entrepreneur, you don't want to be at cross-purposes with divinity.

Jesus issued this instruction to his disciples, instructing him what to do after he ascended to heaven, "Being assembled together with them he charged them, 'Don't depart from Jerusalem, but wait for the gift promised by my father which you have heard me. For John indeed baptized in water but you will be baptized with the Holy Spirit not many days from now." (Acts 1: 4-5)

Indeed, the Holy Spirit soon arrived at Pentecost. Since then, everyone has lived in the "last days" as we do now. In this age, you will be guided by the Holy Spirit in all your work. This means that as a Christian entrepreneur, you will have an exciting opportunity for God to guide you in business activities that fulfill his purpose in some way.

This also means that the entrepreneurial spirit that drives you to achieve what you create -- can sometimes move you in the direction of yourself rather than God. But don't worry! The biblical foundation of the entrepreneurial journey will help you balance the inevitable conflict between your will and God. This will help you continue to adjust yourself to his great plan.

CHAPTER 04:

Focus on target

GOAL SETTING IS an integral part of developing any success-ful and sustainable business. Defining what you want to achieve and how to achieve it will keep you moving forward. Unfortunately, too many business owners have not set realistic goals for their com-panies. Whether your dreams are too big or you don't have a proper attack plan, setting inappropriate goals can kill your business.

If you want to achieve crazy business growth, you need to focus on setting and achieving the right goals for the company. By drawing up an appropriate plan to bring you closer and closer to the expectations you have set for your business you can open up a path of success that doesn't seem impossible.

Why it is essential to improve your business goals

Setting business goals can help any business owner or entre-preneur start the road to success. However, setting ambiguous goals does not support your company to grow. If you do not clearly define the goal to be achieved, you will never know if you are approaching the goal or not.

For example, if your goal is just "business development," you will find it difficult to know if the goal has been successfully achieved. If you do not set parameters, deadlines, and expectations, you will not know what level of growth is sufficient to show that you have reached your goals. On the other hand, you can set specific goals for business growth, such as expected annual income or sales.

Refining and focusing your business goals or targets can give you a flawless path to making a more profitable business. With more precise expectations, you will recognize whether or not your organization is moving in the perfect direction.

Smart Tips to Help You Focus Your Business Targets

Choosing your business goals may seem perplexing at first, but it doesn't need to be problematic. Here are three smart tips that can help you improve your business expectations.

1. Define Your Long-Term Objective(s)

When you first create a company, you may have some ideas for achieving your goals. Whether you want financial success, or to simply help your community, you have aspirations and may be thinking of some of the ultimate goals. However, setting ambiguous long-term goals could make it difficult to know your exact goals.

Defining one or more long-term goals can give you a "finish line." For example, by setting goals for one, five and ten years, you can create a long-term roadmap to help you determine if you're on the right track. First, decide how much money you want to make, how many customers you want to serve, or how many locations you plan to open. These are all good starting ideas for achieving long-term goals.

It may be challenging to think about the future, but remember your goals do not need to be set in stone. If your five-year or ten-year goals no longer align with your values over time, you can always change your expectations as needed. However, drawing up a roadmap for your future development can show you the direction of your work. It will also provide you with guidelines for making decisions or adjusting to unexpected developments.

2. Break your aim into small size chunks

Long-term goals can be overwhelming, and you may not know immediately what steps are needed to reach them. Given the deadline is a future date, you may feel you have enough time to delay achieving this goal. This can mean that eventually you will pass one, five, or even ten years without accomplishing many things.

To make your long-term goals more accessible and manageable, you need to subdivide them into smaller parts. By incorporating a sub-goal, you can reach it more in less time. Your overall goal becomes less overwhelming and you become more motivated to take action every day.

Analyze larger goals by looking at the tasks that need to be completed from one target location and then another target location. Consider the steps you have to take and decide when you need to complete each part to reach a bigger goal in time. Using these smaller goals as stepping stones can enable your company to move toward significant goals and help to track your progress.

3. Make your targets as specific as possible

For many companies, goal setting can become a challenge because they do not set the right parameters. Their ambitions are ambiguous like attracting new customers or selling a particular product, but they haven't set out what they want to achieve. This makes it impossible to know when the goal was reached.

When creating goals, you want to assign specific goals, which will help you determine if each goal has been achieved. SMART goals are specific, measurable, achievable, relevant, and time-based. They give you a clear idea of how much progress you have made in achieving the specific goals. They also make sure your entire team is on the same page and working towards the same objective.

Conclusion

Goal setting, or focusing on the target, doesn't have to be a daunting task. Instead, the aims you establish should serve to move you closer to establishing the successful company you've always dreamed of. When you set higher, yet strong goals, you can continuously grow your business in the right direction.

CHAPTER 05:

Live for Purpose

LIVING FOR PURPOSE is also one of the essential elements of business. If a person doesn't have a purpose in the business, it will be difficult for him to move in the right direction. I studied Scripture to discover a biblical basis for the business' purpose.

Several parts of scripture that are relevant :

» Jesus' pearls of wisdom about the kingdom and his stories about living and growing things.
» The tale of Creation.
» The Lord's orders and examples to Israel were relevant to the economic facets of how they were to live as they toured from Egypt to the Promised Land.
» Paul's lessons about Jesus as the last Adam.

From knowledge of the biblical verses and experience in business, I came up with the top-level purposes for what we as Christians must consider:

» Be a commercially viable company.
» Value humans over money articulated by giving individuals the opportunity to live up to their God-given talent.
» Build up a "respectable place" in communities where people can work.

There's a lot to unload in these three primary purposes.

1. *Be a commercially viable company*

One purpose we should have for the business is that making money should not be the only driving force of the business. Making a profit is essential, of course. We need to meet all our expenditures, repay capital reserves, and, generate extra funds to invest in developments, enhancement, growth, and research.

But our primary purpose for making a profit (which I prefer to call being commercially viable) is to back the other two purposes of the business, which together form its primary purpose.

Allow individuals to live up to their God-given talent

Our business should be known as "Christian business." Give people the opportunity to work with you. As a Christian, you should be the helping hand for people rather than creating hindrances in their path. Also, you need to be very thankful to God for providing opportunities to his people.

Instead of just saying we want people to discover and fulfill Jesus' purpose for their lives while becoming more and more like Christ, we say we should be giving people the chance and inspiration to live up to their God-given potential. Even nonbelievers will overlook the "God-given" part to comprehend that we value individuals and express that significant value through training and development.

In the heart, when I state "live up to your potential" I consider the individual living up to his or her full potential involves becoming more and more like Jesus, and that becoming Christ-like involves accepting Christ as your saviour.

No one needs to be a Christian to work with a Christian. However, we are establishing a corporate culture that enables people to understand the Gospel as a proposition and to spread it in the lives of Christians within the organization. Everyone makes their own decisions from there.

Build up a "Respectable Place" in communities where we work

"Building a good place in the community where we work" is another way of expressing the boundaries in Jesus' prayer. "Your kingdom is here, and you will be completed in earth, just as in heaven." This is not only a clear gospel requirement, but also addresses the needs of widows, orphans and elders. It is the positive life investment opportunity God has given us in this beautiful world created for our lives.

We should learn the cultural empowerment of Bible expression and prosperity to apply these concepts. Regardless of whether people in our business understand or accept biblical views, everyone should work to meet needs and build a good place in the community where people can work with a good heart.

Tying it all together

Monetizing the business allows us to support people's journey to become Christians and express Christ-like style through their impact on our work community. Our high and noble goal of making a profit supports this environment.

The people working with us should be able to see these open religious terms and how they apply to their work. Some people call themselves Christians, while others are secretive Christians. Some are atheists, Hindus, and Muslims. But everybody should be allowed to work together.

Everyone has heard the Gospel. More importantly, everyone experiences the Gospel in a way they understand and can apply to the profitability of the enterprise. Our culture provides compelling reasons for the purpose and use of corporate profits. Like everything in life, despite this, we can still search the Bible and expand our faith-based reasons.

We may find support and go along with how the culture displays us. We may find ways to redeem cultural norms, or we may find something different and better. It all begins with seeking God's view in prayer and Scripture.

CHAPTER 06:

Pray every day before you start your activity

HAVE YOU EVER contemplated why prayer is essential before starting your activity? Wonder no more. Here are the reasons, rooted in truth. Prayer is absolutely imperative!

Reasons why prayer is essential

1. Prayer is essential because it's a form of service

Service is defined as helping or working for someone, providing a system of public demand, or performing routine maintenance or repairs. This is why prayer is important! Because we pray for others. This is how we help others. Prayer can heal emotional wounds. At the heart of prayer is a system that meets the needs of the public. This is the prescribed method for maintaining our mental health.

> "Do nothing from self-centeredness or empty conceit, but
> with humbleness of mind regarding one another as equal to
> ourselves do not just look out for your own personal interests,
> but also for the interests of others." (Philippians 2:3-4).

> The Lord reestablished the fortunes of Job when
> he prayed for his friends, and the Lord increased
> all that Job had by double (Job 42:10).

> "But I say to you, show love to your enemies and pray
> for ones who persecute you (Matthew 5:44).

2. Prayer is imperative because it's an act of obedience

We are asked to pray, and God had designed us for this. It is embedded in our existence. Because we are created in God's image, we must imitate God's behaviour. Jesus prayed to obey the Father's will. Therefore, as an imitator of Christ, prayer must also remain in his will.

> "Before daybreak the next morning, Christ got up and
> went out to a secluded place to pray" (Mark 1:35).

> "My prayer is not for the creation, but for those you have
> given me, because they belong to you" (John 17:1).

> "They all met, collected and were constantly united in
> prayer, along with Mary, the mother of Christ, numerous
> other women, and the brothers of Jesus" (Acts 1:14).

> All the believers dedicated themselves to the apostles'
> teaching, and to fellowship, to and sharing in meals
> (including the Lord's Supper), and to prayer (Acts 2:42).

> Then we apostles can spend our time in prayer
> and teaching the word (Acts 6:4)

3. Prayer is the solution to all the problems

Prayer is an opportunity to resolution, the path to having an answer to a difficulty. It provides a vision to see through our tough decisions and dilemmas.

> Request me, and I will tell you extraordinary secrets you
> do not know about things to come (Jeremiah 33:3).

And so, I tell you, keep on requesting, and you will receive what you request for. Keep on looking for, and you will find. Keep on bashing, and the door will be opened to you. For everyone who requests, receives. Everyone who seeks, discovers. And to everyone who bashes, the door will be opened (Luke 11:9-10).

Then if my disciple who are called by my name will modest themselves and pray and seek my face and turn from their evil ways, I will hear from heaven and will forgive their sins and restore their land. My eyes will be open, and my ears observant to every prayer made in this place (2 Chronicles 7:14).

4. Prayer is imperative because it's a way of communication

Since the beginning, God has been talking to us. We are not always in a place or state where we can hear it. Even Adam and Eve were chatting with their father in the garden before and after sin. He to aspires to share his thoughts, promises, and guidance with us. If you want to communicate with our Lord, you must pray.

Then Lord blessed them and alleged, "Be productive and multiply (Genesis 1:28).

Then the God called to the man, "Where are you?" (Genesis 3:9).

"Who said to you that you were naked?" God asked. "Have you eaten fruit from the tree who I commanded you not to eat?" (Genesis 3:11).

Have the public of Israel build me a holy sanctuary so I can live amongst them (Exodus 25:8).

I am the one who carried them out of the land of Egypt so that I could live amongst them (Exodus 29:46).

5. Prayer is imperative because it's how we make wishes

God pleasures in us. He desires to bless us and shower His favour upon us. When our needs line up with His desires for us, remarkable things happen!

But while praying, walk away, close the door behind you, and then pray to your father in private. In this way, the Heavenly Father who sees everything will reward you (Matthew 6: 6).

The Holy Spirit helped us in our weakness. For example, we
do not know what God wants us to pray for. But the Holy
Spirit prays for us with grow-sings that cannot be expressed in
words. Everyone knows that the Father knows what the Holy
Spirit is saying because the Holy Spirit forces our believers
to be in harmony with God's own will (Romans 8: 26-27).

Yet you don't have what you wish because
you don't ask God for it (James 4:2).

6. *Prayer is imperative as it's how we promote the realm of God*

The greatest sacrifice and devotion is when we set aside our
agenda and accept Christ. When we decide to become less to do
more, God's territory will expand, and the chances of others being
saved will increase. We must pray for this.

"Father, if you are eager, please take this cup of sorrow away
from me. Yet I want your will to be done, not mine" (Luke 22:42).

He told him: "There's one more thing you haven't done
yet." "Go sell all your possessions and give the money
to the poor, and you will have treasure in heaven. Then
come and follow me." The man's face fell. He was sad
because he owned many properties (Mark 10: 21-22).

"If any of you want to be my follower, then you have to
get rid of the selfish way, take the cross every day, and
follow me. If you stick to your life, you will. ' But if you give
up your life for me, you will save lives (Luke 9: 23-24).

7. *Prayer is imperative because it makes us wiser*

The more you distinguish that this isn't just a line in a com-
mercial, it's a broader idea about spiritual living.

The more you recognize, the better equipped you are. The
more you identify, the more prepared you are to make decisions.
The more you understand, the more qualified you become to explain. The more you distinguish, the more you can associate. The
more you see, the better you will differentiate. The more you recognize, the more skillful you will be at defending the Gospel.

Prayer is essential if you want to "know more."

Give me a thoughtful heart so that I can govern
your individuals well and distinguish the difference
between right and wrong (1 Kings 3:9).

We ask Lord to give you complete knowledge of his will and to
give you divine wisdom and understanding (Colossians 1:9).

I pray for you continually, asking God, the glorious Father of our
Lord Jesus, to give you spiritual knowledge and insight so that
you may grow in your knowledge of God (Ephesians 1:16-17).

If you want to have wisdom, ask our generous
God, and he will give it to you (James 1:5).

CHAPTER 07:

Be Self-disciplined

WHEN YOU ARE a new entrepreneur transitioning from 9-5, your daily habits will change a lot to adapt. You can change from the relative structure of daily work (with fixed routines) to making your own rules and taking full responsibility for your own schedule.

One of the main challenges is setting your own deadlines and developing effective strategies around what needs to be done to ensure business goals are achieved. However, without proper self-discipline, it's easy to lose time, live a difficult life, or simply not make progress on the most important and influential tasks in the business.

That's why self-discipline is one of the main skills to develop in order to boost your daily productivity and achieve your immense milestones and daily goals in the business.

Five tips to help you improve your self-discipline

1.   Comprehend that self-discipline needs practice

If you can easily make the transition and wake up on the first day as a new entrepreneur with everything ready and you have a perfect system in place, that would be a great, but the reality is different. It is unlikely to be the case in real life.

Similarly, you do not need to know all the systems and procedures of the new organization to start a new job, but finding the most useful ones in the new role is a skill that requires practice and development. It can take a lot of time. Discover your strengths and weaknesses as a business owner, your best way of working, factors that can increase productivity, and factors that hinder productivity. You should try different methods and have honest conversations with yourself to understand what works for you and what doesn't work for you.

Telling the truth in this way can help to stop you from making up excuses. It can also help you decide when self-discipline is needed; when it's just something you don't like (it's better to delegate it); or when you just are avoiding doing what you really need to do. Give yourself time to develop a system that suits you.

2.   Remember the ratio 80/20 rule

Self-discipline on workload is an integral part of the transition. One of the critical challenges in this area is ensuring that you spend your valuable work time on the tasks that will make your business grow the fastest.

In this case, using the 80/20 rule is a huge advantage. If you have never encountered this explanation before it is called the Pareto principle, which emphasizes the fact that most business owners spend only 20% of their time on the most valuable tasks in their business. And, the remaining 80% is used for trivial activities. Similarly, about 80% of the results in your business come from 20% of the efforts.

As a business owner, your job is to identify and then focus on the 20% of the tasks that really matter. The rest can be delegated, deferred, automated, outsourced, or completely discarded if possible. It may sound difficult to do at first, but once you understand the application of this rule, you will see the benefits in business results and in your life.

3.   *Schedule the most vital task for the beginning of the day*

We have all been in a situation where we are faced with a difficult task, and this is the most important one; it will enable us to get the most benefit. But for some reason, we delay. This can be the task's difficulty, or it can drive us out of our comfort zone. We tell ourselves we will do it after clearing the to-do list, but at the end of the day the essential task is not even started.

We tell ourselves we're going to watch "first thing in the morning." The next day, we just repeat the same pattern and hold it in our head for too long. If you usually postpone tasks like this, one way to solve this problem is to develop a habit of handling tasks.

In simple words, if you have two main tasks before you, start with the biggest, most formidable, and most important task first. Regularly tackling your biggest most significant tasks at the beginning of the day and being disciplined with this practice will augment your productivity hugely.

4.   *A morning routine will enhance productivity*

When you first transition to entrepreneurship, it is easy to get overwhelmed by the many tasks that need to be completed. The idea of going into shortage mode over time and falling into "not enough time in a day" can be tempting.

If you do not use time, then this feeling becomes more apparent. For example, you are unwisely involved in some things—these things will not bring you the most benefit nor will they increase productivity.

Routine morning activities can get you started for a new day and focus on improving work efficiency. Hal Elrod talked about the concept of "accruing habits" in his book "Miracle Morning," which selects a habit from all the daily habits you want to practice and develops a sequence from it so that the new order itself becomes a habit.

This can help you develop good practices and automate your actions to achieve the whole sequence. So, you can use a variety of powerful tools such as meditation and visualization to help you start a new day in a planned way. Starting day like this means you start with the right mindset which is essential for accomplishing a productive day of self-discipline and concentration.

5.   Self-care is the central part of the puzzle

Just as starting a typical day in the morning can help you spend a productive day, prioritizing self-care can also help self-discipline. When you're busy, you can easily skip breakfast, go directly to the computer, or check your email over the phone. Unknowingly, half the day has passed. You've forgotten to eat, feel tired, helpless and start making mistakes. You may think you are working, but most of the time, your attention is drawn to social media.

To get the best results, take some time to rest and schedule mealtimes. When you tell yourself that your brain and body are just as important as the customer and client, it also dramatically improves your self-esteem. Similarly, taking the time to close a company is about achieving self-discipline, productivity, and reducing burnout. For many new entrepreneurs, shutting down is an unfamiliar concept, but many of the most successful entrepreneurs need time daily to close the office door at a certain time. Turning off the power and closing up can help time we spend in business be productive.

A focused and disciplined way of working can ensure the time you spend in business is quality time. In this way, time is allocated for basic self-care tasks. Self-discipline is difficult only if you keep telling yourself it is. Practice it, work hard on important things, and train your own time to see the difference. Finally, self-discipline will bring many gains to business and life.

CHAPTER 08:

Be confident

God has confidence in us

WHEN WE LOOK at the scriptures about self-confidence in the Bible, most of the scriptures we read explain how our faith comes from God. It began when God created the earth and appointed human beings to protect it. God shows over and over again that he has faith in us.

He called on Noah to build an ark. He asked Moses to lead his people out of Egypt, and Esther saved her people from being killed. Jesus wanted his disciples to spread the gospel. The same theme was shown over and over again—God has confidence in us all, to do what he has told us to do. He created each of us for a reason.

So why don't we have any confidence in ourselves? When we put God first, when we focus on the path he is taking on our behalf, he will make everything possible. That should make us all confident.

> "Hence, do not throw away your confidence, which has
> great compensation. For you have need of strength,
> so that when you have done the will of Lord, you may
> receive what was sworn." Hebrews 10:35-36.

What confidence to avoid

Now we know that God has faith in us and that this will be our strength and light and everything we need. However, this does not mean that we are just walking away from all people. We can't just focus on what we need.

We should never think of ourselves better than others if we become stronger, wiser, have money, have a certain race, and so on. In God's eyes, we all receive goals and directions. No matter who we are, we are loved by God. Nor should we rely on the confidence of others. When we trust someone else, when we put self-esteem in the hands of others, we grind.

The love of God is unconditional. No matter what we do, he will never stop loving us. Although the love of others is beautiful, it often becomes lacklustre and causes us to lose faith in ourselves.

> "For it is we who are the circumcision, we who serve God by his Spirit, who boast in Christ Jesus, and who put no confidence in the flesh — though I myself have reasons for such confidence." (Philippians 3:3 -)

Living confidently

When we trust God with self-confidence, we give him power. This can be scary and beautiful at the same time. We have all been hurt and hated by other people, but not by God. He knows we're not perfect, but he loves us anyway. We can have confidence in ourselves because God has confidence in us. We seem ordinary, but God has never seen us that way. We can find confidence in God's hands.

> 1 Corinthians 2:3-5 - "I came to you in weakness—nervous and quivering. And my message and my teaching were very plain. Instead of using clever and persuasive speeches, I trusted only on the control of the Holy Spirit. I did this so you would trust not in the wisdom of humans but the power of God." (NLT)

Many entrepreneurs have particular qualities that are essential for starting and developing businesses. They are passionate, resilient, opportunity-focused, and risk-averse. However, the quality that most affects an entrepreneurs' success is confidence.

If you are confident, you are more likely to discuss your latest business ideas with strangers or promote to new customers effectively. Most of the activities entrepreneurs engage in every day (product launches, critical business decisions, and even board meetings) require a certain level of confidence. If you wish to achieve great success, you must believe you are worth it. Here are some supportive tips to improve your confidence in yourself and your business.

1. Set yourself for success

Be more confident in what you wear. Strive to be well-dressed and able to communicate with others. You want to show people you deal with, that you are a knowledgeable, capable and competent person. When choosing clothes, remember to wear clothes for occasions and the emotional comfort of customers. Before meeting important customers, study the image, office environment, and internal value of their company.

2. Make the correct posture

If your job requires you to sit at your desk for most of the day, your posture is likely to be affected. Don't relax when meeting customers, clients, or colleagues. Poor posture can make you seem unsafe, lazy or miserable. Try to bend your shoulders back and extend your spine consciously. Raise your jaw slightly, keeping your head neutral.

3. Give your best and worry less

Entrepreneurs who lack self-confidence often stress how others see them. Negative self-talk can make you feel as if someone is evaluating every mistake and blunder you just made. Focus on everything you are good at and hire other experts to take care of the rest.

4. Emphasis on the future

If you get caught up in trivial matters in daily affairs, remind yourself to think about your future dreams. If you spend a few minutes focusing on your goals, you can refocus on the aspects that matter most to you and your business.

5. Grip positivity

We have suffered a malicious attack some time in our life. To counteract the negative energy around you (from angry colleagues' comments to the daily news), let your thoughts will be filled with positive thoughts. Thank them for their kindness and express your appreciation to those around you. If you develop positive and grateful habits, it will become second nature.

6. Forget about the small mistakes

Everyone makes mistakes, so don't expect perfection or you'll go crazy. Try not to get caught up in small things. If you make a mistake between yourself and your client, don't be fooled by what you may have done wrong. Instead, take responsibility. Say sorry, fix the error as soon as possible, and move on.

7. Keep on improving

Even if achievements are not directly related to your business, small achievements help build confidence. Learn new skills, take classes at local universities or read books on topics that interest you. If you want to excel in certain areas like golf or public speaking, invest in yourself and take classes.

8. Schedule time to play

If you work 60 to 80 hours a week and never take the time to rest, you will soon be in a state of burnout and fatigue. Make sure you spare some time to do what you like. Take your child or dog to the park, take a lunch break or take a fitness class at the local gym. In addition, if you invest time in your hobbies, friends and family, you will rejuvenate and prepare to overcome the next challenge.

9. Don't hesitate to ask for advice

Whenever you find yourself in an epic battle with self-doubt, call a trusted friend, adviser or colleague and ask for his best advice. An objective perspective will often help you see life in different ways, overcome challenges and change your attitude.

CHAPTER 09:

Avoid laziness

He that observes the wind will not sow; and he that regardeth the clouds shall not gain." (Ecclesiastes 11:4)

PROCRASTINATION CAN INFILTRATE your life, causing you to set aside both the big and the little things you need or want to do. What do you do when you feel the sluggish monster of procrastination trying to sneak into your life?

If you're a meteorologist, there's nothing wrong with spending a lot of time observing wind and clouds. However, if you are a person who observes the wind and clouds to avoid doing the work you need to do, there are many mistakes in doing so. Or, if you feel dormant because you're waiting for the "perfect time," then you might shelve it forever.

Because God understands and is worried about even the most intricate specifics of our lives when we invite Him in, there is hope – even for procrastinators.

Entrepreneurs are lucky in a way that they can pick and set their own time when they need it. This is one of the best benefits of running your own business. However, you must be careful not to take your entrepreneurial freedom for granted and become a lazy business owner.

It's very easy to be a "business owner brand". If you're not careful, you might lie in bed all day and tell yourself you're considering the master plan, or you're repeating the same project over and over for several weeks because of paralysis analysis, or you may constantly be distracted after work. Force divert attention. This self-deception work practice can stall your business. However, you only need to take a few steps each day to get started and take action.

1. Set some time to plan your week.

It only takes 15-30 minutes to write a list and add some steps. You can use Sunday night to create a master task list for next week, which contains everything you need to register, people to contact, and tasks to delegate to team members. Using the "Productivity and Profit Planner", you can prioritize the list so that it can be processed in order of importance, and you won't waste time on trivial tasks. At work, listen to inspirational music or inspirational speeches to help you think in the direction of current projects and dreams.

This list of top jobs makes you focused on the most important things now. Upon completing one task, you must know what to do next. That's why planning in advance will make it easier for you and put everything in order.

Additionally, having a plan helps you track your progress. When you write down what you are doing, you will be able to see where you are lazy and need to get up. You can also find the peak time of the day, as well as high energy time, and lack of energy time. Try to track your daily experience in the "success log". You can use the main weekly task list in the log to track your achievements and reflect on your daily progress. This will give you a deep understanding of your daily work and enable you to improve it.

2. Get up and get dressed

People often underestimate the power of your appearance.

However, when you look good, you feel good and perform well. Dress up for work every day and start each day with intention. You will be put into a work mindset, which will motivate you to work instead of lying in bed too long.

3. Take action.

What are the smallest and most immediate steps you can take to achieve your goal? Do it! Once you start doing something, it's easy to complete a task, and then continue on to complete another task. Avoid the "all or nothing" mentality. Great companies are not built in a day. You do not have to try to do all the work at once. Instead, start with the lowest fruit on the list and work up.

4. Make a daily routine

Instead of letting your day decide on you, it's best to make a structured plan to determine how you want your day. Make a specific benchmark schedule for yourself. When do you wake up? When do you start and finish work? Create the structure that suits you best and then commit to stick to it. You may need to adjust it until you find the ideal rhythm. Check your schedule one night before and after, decide to get up "on time," and start a new day as planned.

5. Change the environment

If you seem unable to improve your work efficiency at home, change the scenery. Take your office to a local coffee shop, where you are surrounded by different people. A productive environment for others will inspire you to increase productivity.

6. Brace yourself to work and win

Before you start your work, surround yourself with everything you need or want. Doing this will avoid having to change your position several times to get them. So, add all the essentials (including snacks) to your desk so you can put in work without having to waste a lot of time.

7. Get organized

A messy environment is very often overwhelming and encourages slow action. Start by cleaning and dusting the work area. It will make you feel ten times better about yourself and inspire you to increase your work efficiency.

8. Get a coach

A business coach will give you updates on business progress. Find someone who you need to answer to and will spur you to take action and keep moving forward in the business. Their clients have a monthly responsibility form to assess progress and set goals for the next month. Reviewing your actions will help you see your productivity and should motivate you to do more.

CHAPTER 10:

Don't give up

DON'T GIVE UP

> Don't give up. No, instead, "Take courage! Do
> not let your hands be feeble, for your work shall
> be compensated" (2 Chronicles 15:7).

Don't give up when that sin still banging at your door after all these years, pounces again with temptation.

> No temptation has passed you that is not common to
> man. God is truthful, and he will not let you be tempted
> beyond your capability, but with the temptation, he
> will also provide the way of forgiveness that you may
> be able to withstand it. (1 Corinthians 10:13)

Don't give up when you feel that intense soul weariness from long battles with ongoing weaknesses.

> "My grace is sufficient for you, for my power is made perfect in
> weakness." Thus, I will claim all the more gladly of my flaws, so
> that the power of Christ may rest upon me. (2 Corinthians 12:9)

Don't give up when your extensive asked-and-sought-and-knocked-for prayers have not yet been answered.

> And he told them (the parable of the persistent
> widow) to the consequence that they ought
> always to pray and not lose heart. (Luke 18:1)

The road to entrepreneurship is exciting. However, sometimes the challenges seem immovable, and some consider quitting. Especially after experiencing several business difficulties,
they began to wonder if they have everything they need. They even
think their innovative ideas are no longer realistic. Self-doubt did
not make them optimistic, but they begin to fall into despair.

Obviously, in any chosen area, the prospect of failing to gain
prominence is painful. However, the good news is that the end
product of the entrepreneurial spirit (an invaluable treasure) should
motivate serious entrepreneurs.

In fact, any serious and creative entrepreneur knows that an
idea that someone cares about takes a lot of time to think about,
worry about, care about, to help it grow and mature — no matter
what measures are taken.

The substitute may not offer any relief

Because most quitters do this out of frustration, there is little
room to consider a contingency plan. For those who continue to develop new businesses, they must deal with the painful reality from
the beginning. Typically, this should not be a problem unless the
early in the business the entrepreneur encounters the same issues
as the previous venture and thus falls back into the same vicious
cycle.

Trials always stand in the way of any business, but the best
thing is that they are there for businesses to overcome, instead of
giving up.

You don't want to be observed as a coward

It takes a process to make a great product, and often this
process is harsh. When a person resigns, he repeatedly states that
the entrepreneur has no money first, which is the process. Having
invested a lot of resources and time into the business, the last im-

pression you want to make is cowardice. Therefore, it is crucial for founders to bear this in mind when entertaining the idea of leaving.

Quitting is the most comfortable option available

In life, there are always easy and challenging paths. Depending on the situation, you will know what to follow. However, one thing is certain about entrepreneurship -- many difficult decisions need to be made. Many times, the founder decides to withdraw completely because the exit seems to be a simple way out.

The founders who are ready to make the hard decisions are of great significance in realizing the true entrepreneurial spirit. It may be necessary to re-prioritize and ask whether true entrepreneurship makes sense to you or whether it is just about paid work.

Achievement is always around the corner

They said that hard work would pay off in the long run. Technically, there is no acceptable basis for measuring hard work or proving that it promotes success. However, in many cases, people think every quality decision and investment made to an idea is to produce the expected results, and this is the goal of continuous progress. Although trials come, you can thrive or persevere in the face of these trials.

In fact, the hardest attempt is the one that comes before the breakthrough. Of course, no one will know this. In most cases, it is difficult to envision a snapshot of the outcome from the start, but it may be even closer than they know to achieve the goal. Quitting it will make the satisfaction of "knowing" disappear.

You don't want someone executing ahead of you

The idea that someone executed faster than you strikes a blow, so taking decisive action is essential. As an entrepreneur, you mistakenly think your ideas are solely yours. Know that there are many participants in entrepreneurial games. When you consider giving up on challenges, others may find the way to put the same ideas into practice.

It may be painful to see others perform in front of you. Even worse, you are surprised to find a small detail that can make the whole thing unique. Then you want to be yourself, and work until you've found a solution to the problem instead of calling it an exit.

Think of the probability of becoming a role model for aspiring entrepreneurs

Mark Zuckerberg, Steve Jobs, and other names are iconic because their stories are a source of inspiration to millions of people around the world. For example, the story of Mark Zuckerberg leaving school to start a business is very popular on the Internet. Although difficult decisions have to be made at some point in life, this hasn't stopped Facebook's founders moving forward and building a multi-billion dollar company.

As an entrepreneur, your hard work and dedication can fuel the dreams of the people around you and even spark the ignition they need to make their dreams a reality. It's nice to know that your story can inspire others. But for those who call it quits, there is never a chance.

In conclusion, every hopeful entrepreneur needs to know the road to entrepreneurship is often bumpy and rocky. Still, with strength of mind they can actually achieve their ambitions.

CHAPTER 11:

Right decision is a key to success

IT CAN BE demanding when you have to make significant decisions regarding your business. We all want to make the correct decisions, and this can create a lot of nervousness. But to get ahead of the game, decisions are a requirement.

Here are some suggestions on how to make the right business decisions.

1. Direction from God

As believers, our overall direction in life is explained by our commitment to God, and we must remember to ask him to direct our lives.

> "Trust in the God with all your heart, and lean not on
> your own understanding; in all your ways recognize
> Him, and He shall direct your tracks" (Proverbs 3:5-6).

How does God guide us? Through the wisdom, he offers us in the Bible and through wise biblical counsel from his people.

We should pray for God's guidance and study the Bible to see what it says about the decisions we face. For example, Proverbs offers many valuable principles. This is a book designed to teach us caution, understanding, and wise decision making (Proverbs 1: 1-4). It all starts with understanding that God is much bigger than us. The fear of God is called the fear of the Lord (v. 7).

When we study the Bible, we should act on what we have learned. We should abandon any choice that is found to be in breach of God's law. Sometimes it is a simple matter of knowing what decision to make - because only one option aligns with obeying God.

But most of our decisions are not so clear. Sometimes there are a few good choices, and sometimes no moral choice is wrong. The following Bible decision-making steps can help us make informed decisions in these situations.

2. Define the problem or opportunity

When our problem looks ambiguous, it is difficult to find a reliable solution.

Sometimes, it may be useful to look at the problem from several angles to define it clearly. What caused the problem to explode now and in this situation? Who is affected by it? If other people's participation is causing problems, why? What do they get out of it?

If your decision is an opportunity, what do you get by choosing it? If you don't choose it, what will you lose? You need to find all the answers to make the right decision.

3. Know all the facts affecting your company

Gather all the necessary facts and information that affect your business. This is essential because you do not want to miss important information which affects how your business operates. In addition, by participating in the information-gathering process, you can eliminate prejudices or opinions others may have.

For example, it is important to understand how your competitors conduct business. Finding ways to increase customer satisfaction is another example of the understanding of companies' facts.

Business owners can talk to their employees and customers to get the necessary information about certain business operations. It is also essential to read all critical business reports and keep up to date with corporate media reports.

4. Target the outcomes

Think about what you need, and consider the possible consequences of the decision. There is a need to focus on the short-term and tall-term goals of all aspects of the company. For example, it is important to keep the company's financial statements up to date. Keeping up with employee morale is another example of setting the direction for the company. Finding ways to improve the company's business approach will significantly help you achieve your business goals and aspirations.

5. Ask around

It's important to consider other points of view besides your own. Ask your friends and business partners for advice. For example, a good way is to talk to your close colleagues and business managers to get their views on how to manage your business. For instance, you must decide whom should control your marketing activities. Ask your business consultant and other managers who they think is best for managing your campaign.

In addition, business personnel can join local business support groups to establish contact with other professionals in the field. This is a great way to gain important information about your industry.

6. Relax

Don't try to do it all at once. When things get busy, stop what you are doing and rest for 10 minutes. Take a deep breath and try to do something that will make you feel relaxed, like walking for 10 minutes, listening to the radio, or doing some stress-stretching exercises. Whether you're dealing with your employees, giving a presentation, or improving the company's marketing plan, you'll feel better and gain a new understanding of your current situation.

7. Stay the path

Managing your own business includes a series of ongoing business decisions. Don't postpone important decisions or worry about your past mistakes — just focus on what's best for the company.

To determine the best results for your business, always listen to your customers' needs and organize your finances and expenses. Customer satisfaction and ensuring company funds are sufficient are essential priorities for any business. If the business is going in the wrong direction, then you need to reassess how your business works.

8. Learn from your mistakes and re-evaluate

If you're doing the wrong strategy, the next step is to get pit there and learn from the mistakes. Learn what you did right and what you did wrong. For example, your company picks a marketing plan for a product but doesn't get the expected sales and customer satisfaction results. When this happens, identify the problem and use this information the next time you sell other products.

CHAPTER 12:

Creating a business strategy

IN THE BUSINESS world, professionals are addicted to tactics because they can help them achieve short-term goals. However, if you focus only on the short term, you will not spend enough time or energy to decide how to succeed in the long run.

Fortunately, developing strategies can help you achieve short-term and long-term goals. A good business strategy results from principles that help you think and goes beyond tactics which implement the plan. It allows you to focus on the reasons why the business carries out certain activities, not just what and how you carry out the activities. Continue reading to understand what the business strategy is and how to build an effective business strategy.

1. Identify your objectives

Identify your business objectives and set aims to measure progress toward achieving those objectives. In business, setting traditional goals allows you to measure your work, but you cannot measure how or why you work. And, if you focus only on the results, it sometimes motivates you to prioritize your organizational needs over customer needs.

To help you focus more on goals and processes than just outcomes, consider and set out your ambitions or vision for your future business. Formulating your business strategy in this way will inspire you to work to serve your customers better. Once the goals are set and accomplished, the goals can be added to the equation, which will help you work on customer-focused tasks and also reach the goals.

2. Identify segments

Identify which segments of your marketplace you want to capture. Your product or service may not be the best product for the entire market, so it is important to determine the market segment that will benefit most from your offerings. The customers who really need and want your products or services will have the longest retention time and are least likely to be lost, which can increase the lifetime value of the customer and reduce customer acquisition costs.

3. Define how you'll beat your competition

The mythical "If you're not the first, you're the last" doesn't necessarily apply to the business world, but it does have some impact. Your customers won't buy two of the same products or services, so if you want to occupy as many market segments as possible, you need to be first in the minds of customers in each segment.

Some of the best ways to stay top-of-mind are making a creatively refreshing brand, distinguishing your product or service from the rest of the crowd, and rating your product relative to its perceived value.

4. Gather the facts

To know where you are going, you must know where you are now. So, before you start looking at the future, you should check your past performance and current situation. Look at the different areas of the business to determine which approaches are practical, which are better, and what future opportunities exist.

Many tools and techniques can can help complete this process, such as SWOT (strength, weakness, opportunity, and threat) analysis. You should look at your strengths and weaknesses from the inside out. For opportunities and threats, you should consider external factors. PESTLE (Politics, Economics, Society, Technology, Law and Environment) is a good framework for studying external factors. So, for your big idea or plan, you ask: what threats and opportunities can appear under each category?

5. Develop a vision statement

The statement should describe the future direction of the business and its medium and long-term goals. This is about defining the purpose and value of the organization. The business experts have had a long and laborious debate on the basic goal (vision or mission statement). However, in reality, you can develop both at the same time.

6. Develop a mission statement

Like the vision statement, a mission statement defines the goals of the organization but also outlines its primary objectives. This looks at what needs to be done in the short term to achieve a long-term vision. So, for the vision statement, you might need to answer the following question: "What do we want to be in 5 years?" For the mission statement, you need to ask the following questions:

» What do we perform?
» How do we conduct it?
» Who are we doing it for?
» What value does our product bring?

7. Identify strategic objectives

At this stage, the task is to create a set of high-level goals for each area of the business. They need to emphasize priorities and inform the plan to ensure the vision and mission of the company are realized. By reviewing the comments in the first step, especially the

SWOT and PESTLE analysis, you can incorporate the strengths and weaknesses identified in the target.

Crucially, your goal must be SMART (specific, measurable, achievable, realistic and time-dependent). Your goals must also include factors such as KPI (key performance indicators), resource allocation, and budget requirements.

8. Identify required competencies

Unfortunately, passion is not enough to beat your competitors and develop into an industry leader. Talent and skills are just as important. Based on your ambitions, goals and market, find out what types of teams and employees you need to develop and recruit, not only to defeat your competitors but also to stay successful.

9. Decide on the management systems

If your business is a team, then your manager is the coach. Upper management is responsible for developing, supporting and inspiring employees to do their best. Because no matter how many original talents your employees have, they will not realize their potential without coaching. If they do improve the skills and discipline necessary for competition and success, they will help companies realize their potential, too.

10. Principles over tactics

We live in an age where the internet is full of suggestions. You can find countless tips and tricks that could help you build a successful business. However, if you so not discern whether these techniques apply to your particular situation, you will never be able to achieve long-term success.

Therefore, strategy is so essential today. It bases your business on principles that can be applied to almost any situation, and in turn, helps your business achieve short-term and long-term goals.

11. Performance management

All plans and hard work may have been completed, but it is

essential that all goals and action plans are reviewed often to ensure you continue to achieve your overall goals as planned. Managing and monitoring the whole strategy is a complex task, which is why many directors, managers, and business leaders are looking for alternative ways of dealing with strategies. Managing and reviewing strategies requires gathering information; breaking down the data; sorting what is relevant, prioritizing, updating plans; and having a clear strategic vision.

CHAPTER 13:

Be patient

FROM A VERY young age, we are told patience is a virtue. However, few of us can show or learn how to be patient. We are impatient; this is something we do unconsciously. Patience is like any other hard discipline: the more we practice, the more patient we become.

To succeed in reaching our strategic goals, we need to be patient with employee relations, how we conduct business, and in our communications. In addition, we must remain calm in the turbulent times life brings. Just by waiting patiently, we can learn from the curve balls thrown our way.

Here are the benefits of practicing patience:

1. Positive rewards

Some people are impatient, and some are patient. When we don't show patience, we are unable to delay satisfaction for more than a moment, which makes us frustrated. Frustration is the expressive energy that fuels "quitting." When we behave impatiently, we are unable to work towards our business goals in a committed fashion. We begin to quit and to start over, and we run this pattern over and over again.

Changing habits requires strong motivation. We must ensure

we are rewarded by taking mature countermeasures. Patience can reward us with positive recognition, more sales, higher customer satisfaction, more substantial profits, or the improvements we seek. No matter what the realization is, it comes from the sum of patience and hard work.

2. Smart decision-making

When making an informed decision, patience is your most powerful resource. Many business people are looking for competitive advantages and ways to improve performance. It is good, but not enough. Don't let the illusion break, thinking that a keen business plan and the best talent can replace the benefits needed to lead and guide the business in the right direction.

Patience is one of those qualities. When we behave patiently, we stay out of the negativities that can cloud our judgment. "Whatiffing" ourselves with catastrophic outcomes is typically human but also totally destructive to our capacity to make good decisions. By behaving patiently, we have the mindfulness to stop and emphasize the present moment. By being in this moment, we can make wise choices that include the big picture.

3. Build reputation

Successful people in business differentiate themselves by mastering the skills that lead to success. Patience gives us courage. It enables us to work consistently towards our goals. When we regularly achieve our goals, we build a reputation. Unwavering faith is the foundation on which a reputation is built.

It is when we continue, despite the difficulties, that we accomplish the higher levels of success we seek. Any attempt that could possibly become a great success requires us to commit ourselves to a long, hard effort. This is only possible when we are patient with our improvement, no matter how fast or slow it goes. So, be the last executive/company standing, and others will see you as responsible, reliable, and their first choice for someone to conduct business with.

4. Self-possession

Patience puts us in straight control of ourselves. And there is no more influential aid to success than self-possession. When we behave patiently, we offer ourselves time to choose how to reply to a given event instead of getting emotionally hijacked by our feelings. Patience allows us to stay gathered, no matter what happens around us. With self-management, we build faith in our capacity to deal with whatever comes our way.

Lack of success or progress can almost always be attributed to a lack of patience. The most fundamental reason for the lack of patience is the lack of control. When we have no control, we lack understanding and insight. When we lack understanding and insight, we lack the ability to plan, communicate and set realistic expectations. However, when we manage these tasks, we get the reward that can bring patience.

5. Tolerance

With the help of patience, we can increase our tolerance. It gives vision; we can anticipate roadblocks and deal with them diplomatically. When we expect challenges, we will respond with extraordinary courage, strength, and optimism. We know that emotional discomfort is part of any obstacle. We accept that the curve of life is a natural part of the business cycle; therefore, I would not add any other pain, suffering, or revenge to this fight. Instead, we roll up our sleeves to do the work we needed to do.

6. Hope

Patience brings hope. It keeps us constantly updating our beliefs about the goals we expect and the heights we are trying to achieve. When we are full of hope, we have the natural resilience and willingness to keep trying because we believe in the possibility of achieving good results. With our success, we will slowly but surely understand that delay does not mean denial.

7. Positive team culture

Patience yields higher results. The focus and emphasis of any business, leader, or company should be their cultural attitude or emotional tone. If our corporate culture is correct, then all the other elements necessary for success (such as excellent customer service) will happen. A culture of engagement can only be formed through patient dedication to the goal you want to achieve.

8. Excellence

Patience develops excellence. Talent is the patience acquired over time. At the heart of every true success is an understanding of the difficulties inherent in any achievement and valuable confidence in the belief that perseverance and patience will be needed and realized. In this way, genius is nothing more than a person being patient.

We patiently realize our potential. Through patience, we can provide the world with a unique sign of our excellence. This is not a trivial matter because the world desperately needs the best we can provide.

CHAPTER 14:

Believe in what you do

You must have faith in what you do.

BELIEVING IN WHAT your business does might seem trivial, but the fact is it can make a significant difference. Like the quote mentioned above states, it makes you much more powerful than those who just have an interest.

Here are the three most prominent reasons why you must believe in what you do:

1. Believing gives you the motive to start

In many cases, the hardest part of doing something is getting started. Inertia must first be overcome. After overcoming the difficulty starting, things become simple. Your beliefs can help you overcome lethargy. If you believe in your job, then there are good reasons to start and you have every reason to overcome any obstacles. Only then can you start doing difficult things.

2. Believing aids in spreading the word to others

When you believe in what you are doing, you are full of enthusiasm. People will feel it when they meet you. They can feel your energy and passion. As a result, they are more likely to believe your information. On the other hand, if you don't believe what you're doing people can easily dismiss you. After all, there are many other things that need attention. Why are they listening to you? Your faith makes you stand out.

3. Believing keeps you enthused during difficult times

This is probably the most important benefit of having a firm belief in what you are doing. Whether you like it or not, hard times are inevitable. You can work hard, but the results may not be good, or you may encounter unexpected obstacles. So, prepare yourself to face the unexpected and believe in your work.

Your beliefs determine an essential part of your life. They give you a basis for decision making, determine your reaction to different situations, and even affect the way you interact with people around you. This applies to any kind of faith, political, religious, or philosophical. It is important that you recognize that your internal beliefs influence your decisions so you can adapt or at least consider them.

There are some beliefs which could make you a more successful entrepreneur: These beliefs can often empower people, drive them to work harder, and allow them to make better decisions while resisting obstacles.

Here are some of those empowering beliefs:

1. Everything is possible

If you think you will never be able to create a multi-million-dollar business, then you will never expend any effort to create a business. If you feel that your business can't compete with the major players, you will lose enthusiasm and eventually go bankrupt under pressure.

Belief that some things are impossible to solve becomes a self-fulfilling prophecy; on the contrary, the mindset of a successful business owner is that as long as enough information, energy, and determination are invested, everything is possible. Having the confidence to move ahead is half the battle, and as long as this action doesn't turn into stubborn arrogance (more on that later), it will make you work harder and set greater goals.

2. Hard work pays off, even if it takes years to see

Successful business owners also believe, fundamentally, that hard work pays dividends. They are not afraid to put hours, weeks, months or even years of hard work into their business, because they firmly believe the results will be valuable.

The main difference for successful entrepreneurs is that they can imagine and receive long-term returns. This ability is known as delayed gratification, and at one time, theoretical physicists called it "a sign of human intelligence."

3. It doesn't have to be perfect

Even experts always make mistakes. If you are a perfectionist, you will suffer many types of torture: you set your goals too high, and if you fail to reach your goals or make mistakes, you will feel frustrated and unsatisfied. Despite one or two pitfalls, successful business people are still ready to move forward.

If you wait until everything is perfect before releasing a product or making a decision you will never succeed, which is why it's important to start with the least viable product and gradually improve it. Forgive your mistakes, learn from them, and don't let them stop you from taking the next step.

4. It's not possible to do everything alone

Even if you have created incredible achievements based on your own efforts, it is still because the people in your life have taught and supported you. That's why you have the maximum achievements. Even in things like building social followers you have to rely on outsiders to help support your enterprise, and in this, you always rely on others. The trick is to do what you can and then surround yourself with the most talented, capable, and respected people to help you care for others.

5. Risks are compulsory

Not all risks are identical, and not all risks are worth taking. Still, if people are divided into risk-takers and non-risk-takers, statistically speaking, there are far fewer risk-takers. Leading and successful entrepreneurs know not to take all the risks they discover, but they are not afraid to take planned risks, which gives them greater potential for larger schemes and to become more successful.

6. Experience and perspective matter

Successful entrepreneurs know that they are not the most intelligent, most experienced, or most reasonable people in the world. They recognize other business owners have more experience, have different perspectives, and may have valuable ideas or insights they have not considered. Successful entrepreneurs show humility and will not feel ashamed to seek help, and will not hesitate to seek the views of others. They are ready and eager to gather information from many sources before moving on.

7. There's always something extra to learn

Humility also extends to this belief. No matter how long you go to school, how many courses you've taken, or how many years you've spent working, there's new information about your industry and the world. Keeping your desire and initiative to pursue your education indefinitely can keep you sharp during the whole entrepreneurial process and keep you ahead of your competitors.

It is challenging to redefine your belief system, especially when your assumptions are deeply rooted. Still, if you can incorporate these beliefs into your internal philosophical system, you will have a greater chance of becoming a successful entrepreneur.

CHAPTER 15:

God gave you the opportunity to manage, be trustful

GOD WANTS YOU to make an effort so that others will see Him in your work. When you act with integrity, you do your best. God wants you to do the right thing, even if no one is checking on you. Proverbs 16:11 (NIV) calls it a "degree of honesty."

Based on Proverbs 16:11, here are some reasons why "honesty" is essential in God's business.

1. *Business is God's work*

When individuals exchange goods and services for money, transactions are grounded on relationships based on trust. People need to know there will be a fair exchange for doing business together. Otherwise, the foundation of the relationship will collapse, and no transactions will be made.

In biblical times, people used scales and weights to determine the value of something. Today, at a grocery store, when we weigh produce, we assume the scale is correct, and often certified. However, in biblical times God condemned traders who had two weights, one for buying and one for selling. We are to have "honest standards."

There is no doubt that you have done business with a company and felt you were being used. Losing trust makes you feel to not trust them again. As a result, you no longer want anyone to do business with them. You don't want to be used again, nor do you want anyone else to encounter the same situation. People instinctively know that fairness should operate in a business environment. God ordained it that way and wrote that law in your heart. Because, your business is God's business.

God's way or the highway

God cares about you and everyone else on this planet, enough to care about how you do your job. God is very interested in the way we work. He wants to point others to your work. So, let the profession you choose indicate that you have chosen to follow God.

God wants you to treat your business as His business. He wants you to run your business as God's business. That's because he wants people to see trust in action. God wants you to conduct business transactions in the way that people see him. He hopes to trade in a trusted environment to deepen relationships between people. It is not about getting the most out of the transaction. You are to represent God in all your business activities.

God is not interested in deceiving others. This leads to the fragmentation and rupture of social structures. God wants his way of doing business to protect ourselves. God puts us on a narrow path so we can enjoy our relationship with others more. He hopes our business transactions will bring us closer together, not farther apart. He wants you to have an "honest standard" so you trade with your peers in a mutually beneficial way.

Every business belongs to Him

Your business is not actually your business. The business you own is essentially God's business. He owns everything—because

He owns it all. He has given you the opportunity to manage. So, have faith in him. Just do your best and leave the rest to him. He is the owner of the cattle on a thousand hills (Psalm 50:10). The world and all its richness are his (Psalm 24:1; Psalm 50:12; Psalm 89:11).

When you realize you don't actually own your property, everything will look new. You don't own your business; you are just the administrator. The business belongs to him. This means you have to give it to him anyway because he is your boss. Not only does your business have an "honest balance", he owns the location of your company, he owns your business operating space. God even owns the air you breathe.

As the Scripture states, "in Him, we move and live and have our being" (Acts 17:28). That includes what you do every day. God is not renouncing the business sector: business is all about relationships—and God is all about associations. As some said, "There is not a square inch in the whole domain of our human existence over which Jesus, who is Sovereign over all, does not call, 'Mine!'" And that includes your business because it's ultimately God's business.

How to manage this opportunity from God

God wants us to help and bless others.

In 1 Peter 4:10, we are required to use our gifts to serve others and to become faithful stewards of the grace of God. Now, in this case, Peter speaks of spiritual gifts such as prophecy and healing. These are the supernatural abilities God has given to all who follow Christ, but the general idea of blessing others can also be extended to talent. God will give us nothing for solely our own benefit. After all, we are blessed (Genesis 12: 2)!

God wants us to form his kingdom for his glory.

God makes us all different. That's great because we all form the kingdom together. In 2 Corinthians, 12:1 Paul compares the body of Christ with the body of humans: we are all unique, but together we make the body complete. Jesus is the head of the body (Ephesians 5:23), so everything we do defers to him. He directs everything!

In simpler words, God wants you to play your unique role in the body of Christ to honour him. So, if God made you an amazing singer, sing to him. If your talents are less traditional (you may be good at numbers or writing code), then you can find a way to turn your talent into work, or volunteer work, in a company or ministry that worships God. Use your God-given ability to reach those who don't know him, and credit him with your talents.

"'Jesus said to him you shall love the Lord your God with all your heart and with all your soul and with your mind.' This is the first and second and great commandment. A second likewise is this, you shall love your neighbour as yourself. The whole law and the prophets depend on these two commandments" (Matthew 22:37–40). When we use the opportunities we are given, to honour Him and to bless others, we're doing just that.

God wants us to trust him

To complete the winning formula, the last cornerstone is your trust in him. This requires that you to trust him and follow him. When you believe in his promises, you will be able to follow his business practices, and your soul will establish a bond of trust.

> "Thus, says the Lord: Cursed is the man who trusts in man and makes flesh his strength, whose heart departs from the Lord. For he shall be like a bush in the desert, and shall not see when good comes, but shall populate the parched places in the wilderness, in a salt land which is not inhabited." (Jeremiah 17:5-6 NKJV)

Unfortunately, as problems arise, people rely more on social systems and technologies than on God, which leads to disappointment, losses of finances, family, friends, and even the business itself. Trust means we believe and rely on him in the presence of business or individuals, no matter what happens. We cannot say we believe in God but refuse to accept and follow his principles, which will lead to change and reform. The Bible says, "Is there anything difficult for the Lord?" If you dare to believe in God, there is no limit to what God can do, and what he will do.

CHAPTER 16:

Follow your eternal instinct

Everyone experiences intuition. From personal safety to decision-making and interpersonal relationships, intuition nudges us. These intuitive clues are provided to us in many forms and rarely mislead us. In my experience, intuition is a combination of wisdom, experience, and feelings. Prudent entrepreneurs will listen to their inner voice, while others will not even admit to them or deny their ability to inform. These insights can be helpful.

What is intuition?

A rational explanation of intuition may help to see things as providing an additional perspective. Your intuition is based on past experiences, opinions and accumulated knowledge. Powerful and intuitive abilities cannot replace logic and analysis needs; it complements our ability to make informed decisions. We cannot access the information stored in the brain within a nanosecond. However, our intuition kicks in without any thought or intention to intervene. Even if we do not remember the source of the information, intuition provides a lot of input.

Intuition is neither nonsense nor magic

As the famous businessman Steve Jobs said, "Have the daring to follow your heart and intuition. They somehow already know what you genuinely want to become. Everything else is secondary."

According to research distributed by Project Management Degrees, only 50% of Americans believe that their intuition can tell them the truth. Moreover, only 62% of corporate executives often rely on instinct. It takes courage to believe in your intuition, but it takes more courage to admit to others how much you rely on intuition. I think this is because many people make false assumptions about intuition, thinking that this is a magical phenomenon, a lie, or it just exists in the minds of crazy individuals.

Why should logic overrule intuition?

Another businessman, Richard Branson, said, "I rely far more on gut instinct than researching huge amounts of statistics."

Have you ever made an important decision based on whether you really want something? However, your inner feelings do not match the logic you are trying to apply to the decision. People often ignore fear and push out the feelings of anxiety. I think we all do this, and we usually regret our actions, eventually.

It is wise to review financial and business decisions with research and logic processes, but these alone cannot tell the whole story. When making a decision, you may be intuitive about the people involved, or you will be reminded by the subconscious that you do not have the necessary time or skills. There is a lot of information kept in your subconscious, which will bubble at the right time.

How to connect with your intuition?

Physical sensing is the most powerful way to connect with your intuitive voice. The rapid emergence and disappearance of ideas also is often the result of your instinct at work. Sometimes, there may not be clear connections but just an image or a feeling.

Some people may even experience mild physical symptoms such as headaches, indigestion or discomfort, muscle or heart pain.

Some tips on how to follow your instinct

Sit in silence

Important decisions deserve a quiet time. Sit down with your eyes closed and listen to ideas related to the topic. Write them down and let your thoughts go in your diary or notebook. Exploring your thoughts will yield some insights. It may take some getting used to. Keep a journal to track your intuitive results; this will help you learn to trust your instinct.

Distinguish between fear and intuition

Some of the messages you receive may be fear speaking; some are from your heart. How do you tell the difference? You just need to ask your body. Stand up and state your decision as you have already made it.

"I am going to buy this new business."

Now, scan your body. Do you feel positive enthusiasm, such as feelings of happiness in your heart and a soaring sense?

On the other hand, do you feel like the world is crashing down on you? Does your chest or stomach feel tight or constricted? Again, note down these feelings and see where it takes you.

Now stand up and state the opposite and see what happens.

"I am not going to buy this business."

How does that feel different? Write about everything you notice.

Follow your gut. The greatest businesspersons trust their intuitive instincts; there's no reason you can't do the same.

Does it have any connection with Science?

"Trust your instincts" is an ancient suggestion, but also seems to be a reasonably scientific suggestion. If your brain makes decisions, what does your intuition have to do with it? There are a few factors to consider behind gut trust, which are rooted in sound research, neuroscience, and psychology.

Why are some things you remember effortless, while others require you to think really hard? The reason is that your mind has two kinds of memory: explicit memory and implicit memory, with the latter viewed as the driving force for Gut sensation.

Explicit or specific memory is information that you have to focus your work on without delay. If you've ever studied a test, it's a clear reminder for you at work. However, implicit memory is everything that gets stuck in your head with no conscious effort. Think of implicit memory as the explanation for how you can randomly call movie quotes and song lyrics after watching a movie or listening to a song. You don't think about it; the brain absorbs it.

When implicit and explicit memory functions work together, you gain mature skills that gradually develop into a second nature. For example, you have to learn to ride a bike specifically, but this skill will benefit you for life once you learn it. Your implicit memory reminds you how to balance, step forward and manipulate the specific memory of the past. You do not need to learn how to ride a bike every time you ride a bike.

With the help of implicit memory, you realize touching a hot stove is a bad idea, or falling in love is fun but possibly harmful to your heart. These implicit memories can help develop your gut instinct which can guide you to better decision-making founded on past triggers you may not even recall with your conscious mind.

In primal situations, it was the gut response caused by our simple implicit memory that often saved us. These unconscious queues help evoke memories of danger and help preserve life.

Although most situations today are not life and death situations, gut instinct still has important meanings and can be learned from your life experience. These instincts will usually tell you something you should pay attention to, or at least admit and explore before making a decision.

CHAPTER 17:

Do a life inventory

A "LIFE INVENTORY" will assist you in analyzing your personal characteristics in many categories. Thinking about the facets of your life and then writing them down on paper requires time and energy, but you will undoubtedly get out of the experience as much as you put into it.

First, you analyze your global identity. Your worldly identity is made up of things shared by unbelievers and believers, such as roles, gender, temperament and legacy. Next, you switch to thinking of your identity as a believer, you focus on personal values. Your identity in heaven is the result of your trust in Christ.

What to include in our inventories?

Honesty

In John 8:31-59, Jesus is involved in a heated discussion with people about who he is. At one point, he says to them, "You are offspring of your father, the devil, and you love to do the evil things he does. He was a murderer from the start. He has always unloved the truth, because there is no certainty in him. When he lies, it is constant with his personality; for he is a liar and the father of lies" (John 8:44).

In Luke 16:10, Jesus says to his disciples, "If you are authentic in little things, you will be faithful in large ones. But if you are dishonest in tiny things, you won't be truthful with greater responsibilities."

Many times, we shade the truth. Other times, we're just plain deceitful. When we are stunned by our problems we lie, not only to ourselves but to others.

Purity

In Mark 7:15, Jesus states,

> "It's not what goes into your body that despoils you; you are despoiled by what comes from the heart." His followers didn't understand, so Christ explained his arguments. "Can't you see that the food you put into your body cannot despoil you? Food doesn't go into the heart, but only passes through the belly and then goes into the sewer" (Mark 7:18-19).

He clarified that the Jewish food laws were no longer in force—the issue now was related to the heart. In the Sermon on the Mount, Jesus states,

> "God blesses the individuals whose hearts are clean, for they will see God" (Matthew 5:8). Later in that same sermon, he gives a hard statement about purity: "If your eye—even your good eye—causes you to lust, gouge it out and throw it away. It is healthier for you to lose one part of your body than for your whole body to be thrown into hell" (Matthew 5:29-30).

These are Jesus' harsh words, but they show how behavioural purity, including sexual purity, becomes part of our lives when we prioritize the will of God to our own.

Start a new inventory page and write "Purity" at the top. Make sure you think about life as part of the checklist.

Unselfishness

Jesus told the followers,

"Among you, it will be diverse. Whoever wishes to be a leader among you must be your servant, and whoever wishes to be first among you must be the slave of everybody else. For even the Son of Man came not to be helped but to assist others and to give his life as a payoff for many" (Mark 10:43-45).

If we are to live an authentic Christian life, we must learn to change from our selfish way. For this, we must face reality and honestly search for the proud list in our hearts.

Launch the "selfless" page. How did you take selfish actions, and how did this affect the individuals in your life? One of the most selfish behaviours is trying to control others, so include its actions in your list.

Love

There is a lot of misrepresentation today in our culture about love. For many people, it is just a feeling. But to look at love as a whole, we must go beyond emotions and feelings. We must describe love by our behaviours.

John 13:1-5 starts with the story of Jesus and the followers preparing their Passover meal in the upper room. John expresses us that Jesus:

"It was before the special religious gathering to remember how the Jews left Egypt. Jesus knew the time had come for Him to leave this world and go to the Father. He had loved His own who were in the world. He loved them to the end. He and His followers were having supper. Satan had put the thought into the heart of Judas Iscariot of handing Jesus over to the leaders of the country. Jesus knew the Father had put everything into His hands. He knew He had come from God and was going back to God. Jesus got up from the supper and took off His coat. He picked up a cloth and put it around Him. Then He put water into a wash pan and began to wash the feet of His followers. He dried their feet with the cloth He had put around Himself." (13:1-5 NLV)

When the pupils arrived at the house to eat the Easter meal, servants were to wash their feet because they came in from the dusty road. Rather it was because they have not yet grasped the concept of loving each other. They are all sitting there with their dirty feet and when Jesus came in, he became their servant and washed their feet to show his love for them. He showed his love through his actions.

When you start the list page of "Love" at the top, you'll find many ways that you can show love. Seek out ways to show love by serving others rather than being served.

Honesty, purity, selflessness, and love: these are the four fundamental elements of a fulfilling life. I know this is a serious challenge, but we can do this. We can choose to stop defending our actions and improve on them. Give this process to your beloved Heavenly Father and enjoy the healing and restoration that comes with a life of repentance and confession of sin.

Managing your business inventory

A good inventory management process means you can quickly determine inventory by hand and its value. Understand the types of inventory you have and how to manage items so that there is enough inventory.

What is inventory in business?

Inventory is the goods and materials acquired, produced or manufactured by an enterprise for manufacture, sale or exchange. Inventory management is part of supply chain management and can help you make sure the right product is available in the right quantity at the right time.

Having an up-to-date inventory list can help you maintain inventory levels and better understand sales and non-sales. This can help you reduce costs and increase sales. It can also help you meet your tax obligations, as all businesses must consider the value of their trading stocks at the end of each income year (end of period stock) and at the beginning of the financial year.

Categories of inventory

Categorizing and classifying your inventory can benefit your business plan and budget of your business.

There are three main categories of inventory:

» raw materials
» work-in-process
» finished goods

The inventory doesn't comprise capital assets such as:

» company cars used to visit customers
» equipment and tools for the business
» staff and training requirements

How to manage your business inventory

When you have inventory to look after, you need to strike a balance between how much to purchase to satisfy clients' needs, with how much inventory is at risk of getting old or not required.

To manage your inventory efficiently, these four points can help:

1. Evaluate what you have now
2. Review what you had
3. Analyze sales
4. Identify items to repurchase or retire

1. Evaluate your inventory

When evaluating inventory, you will need an inventory recording system that can track the size of your existing materials or products. Make sure your recording system records the inventory you actually own.

If you use a periodic inventory system, records will be periodically updated by physically counting each item. If a permanent inventory system is used, the record will be updated immediately after changing the inventory level. These systems are usually electronic and linked to the point-of-sale system.

2. Assess your last inventory stock-take

When you have a list of items in the inventory, use your prior inventory item list and compare statistics. You may want to consider:

» Have figures stayed the same?
» Have figures increased?
» Do you have stock that is not important?
» Is there stock that is not selling?

3. Check sales

When comparing inventory listings, you should also review sales data. Using these three documents (current inventory list, previous inventory list and sales list), you will be able to identify and decide which items:

» sell rapidly after you purchase them
» haven't sold well
» are essential to your business

Sales of core business products are stable and provide significant gross profit. Remember that seasonally sold items can sell slowly for the rest of the year.

4. Identify items that you need to repurchase or discard

You should now be able to decide which items to buy on a regular basis and which items to discontinue.

Discontinuing some items will provide more space in your storage unit and for other items on display. When unable to return goods you will need to sell the remaining inventory. You may wish to consider selling these at a discounted price.

When repurchasing, consider whether you need to increase the order size. If the product sells fast, you can reduce shipping costs by ordering more products. You can also order more regularly and arrange more frequent deliveries.

CHAPTER 18:

Fitness limits your ability? Foolishness?

LIFE AS AN entrepreneur is very busy. Sometimes it seems you don't even have time to eat or breathe deeply. It is crucial to maintain your health and well-being while working on your dreams. A little willpower will balance life, fitness, and work.

Make a reasonable schedule

It is ideal to maintain a schedule that suits your business and personal needs. This means you should plan specific working hours and observe them. Organize the rest of your time for your own purposes. The schedule should only be broken when absolutely necessary.

In your schedule, take some time for:

All of these elements are important and need to be built into your schedule. When there is regularity in your life, you can maintain a healthy lifestyle and stay healthy. At some point during the day, take some time to disconnect from the technology and relax. Once you have developed these new habits, you will feel uncomfortable breaking your schedule.

Plan time to workout

Staying active helps improve overall health, including mental health. Organize daily exercise time before or after work. Change the daily exercise routine to exercise different parts of your body. This helps to shape your whole body and ensure you exercise all muscle groups equally.

Consider hiring a personal trainer to design a weekly exercise program for you that aligns with your personal goals. Goal setting can help you build a stronger work ethic and maintain motivation to exercise daily. Ask your personal trainer about the exercises you can do in a hotel room on a business trip or other accommodation a gym facility is not available.

Keep your exercise plan during weekends and holidays. Break the routine, and your body will notice. Exercise increases adrenaline energy, allowing you to get up fast or relieve stress after work.

Consume a balanced diet

A proper diet is a critical factor in maintaining health. The day should begin with a delicious protein-rich breakfast. Protein helps in maintaining energy and helps you stay focused. Make your own lunch or visit only healthy restaurants.

To help you maintain a healthy diet, consider working with a dietitian to develop a customized diet plan for your physical needs and to evaluate what you enjoy eating. The meal plan should be used as a guide to help you shop and prepare meals. Fresh meat, fruits and vegetables need to be at least two-thirds of your diet. Avoid processed, fried and high-fat foods.

Part of the meal plan is possibly going to include cutting down on cocktails. Alcohol slows the body's digestion and often leads to feeling off the next morning. It is also one of the leading causes of missed morning workouts.

Keep your roster while travelling

Although jet lag can make it difficult to keep up with your

daily work, you still have to do this. Keep your schedule at home when you travel. Use the exercise option in the hotel room so you can at least do some form of exercise if you can't maintain your full daily exercise plan.

Get sufficient sleep

Sleep is something you should consider more seriously. First, go to bed at the same time during the week. Set the alarm every night and get up at the same time every morning. Your body needs some regularity to help your internal clock.

A fresh, rested brain can make better decisions. If you have difficulty relaxing before falling asleep, try some sleeping pills or go for a walk. A walk helps to relax the body and mind so you can get the right amount of sleep-time and can perform your professional duties as well as possible.

Learn to cope with stress

As an entrepreneur, buildup of pressure is almost inevitable, but it can be resolved. The important thing is that you learn to control your thinking and decision-making process. Not only is stress detrimental to your personal health, but it can also have a negative impact on your business.

Stress has the possibility of ruining relationships with clients, the ones you have currently and future ones to come. Stress is the last thing your business wants, so learn to cope with it and keep it at bay during critical times. Stress doesn't fade away with more success, as many would like to think. As a matter of fact, it's often the opposite. Stress is never going to disappear completely, so learn how to manage it as best as possible. Take time to unplug from the business and relax

Doing business is full of stress. If you do not spend time relaxing and unplugging the power cord from time to time, you will suffer from burnout. Many entrepreneurs believe they have to work non-stop. Your business can be really is time consuming, but you must know when to relax and recharge.

Take time out of your weekly schedule to devote to hobbies. Playing golf, fishing, watching movies, or doing anything else that will relax you. Family time is also an excellent way to escape and unwind. And, don't be afraid to go on vacation occasionally. Time spent travelling can be very beneficial – time spent with the family is always the best time.

Conclusion

It's vital to invest time in maintaining yourself. Sleep, diet, exercise, and resting are essential to growth and well-being. You do not have to commit to long workout sessions. Studies have proven exercise bursts of 5-10 minutes several times a day can be successful. When you are satisfied with your health, you can balance your life and live according to your plan.

CHAPTER 19:

Organize your daily life

THE ORGANIZED FOLKS are not born organized; they have cultivated these habits over time, which then helps them to stay organized for the rest of their lives.

Even if you believe you are a very disorganized person, you can become and stay organized. Scheduling, jotting things down, scrapping the unnecessary stuff from your life are just steps, but they will help you become an organized individual as long as you're enthusiastic about learning and practicing.

Here are the necessary habits on how to organize your daily life:

1. Make a list

We all know someone who remembers every birthday and sends cards every holiday. This is not magic; they are not using memory. Trying to remember things will not help you stay organized. You should write it. Pen and paper are the way we remember things externally, and they are more durable. You can also use the powerful digital brain in your device.

By keeping appointments and reminders in mind, you will only make life more complicated. Write down everything: food shopping lists, holiday gifts, home décor, and important dates, such as meetings and birthdays. As an experiment, try to write their names shortly after meeting someone (when they are away). I'm sure you'll remember more names like this.

2. Make schedules and deadlines

Organized people do not waste time. They recognize that keeping the organization organized and maintaining productivity are closely linked. They develop and maintain a daily and weekly schedule. They set deadlines and set goals. The most important thing is that they have to persevere! Similarly, with a messy lifestyle, you will not have the time or space to meet deadlines or achieve goals.

As an experiment, check your bucket list or create one. Write down what you want to achieve this year in life. Then write down what you need to do to achieve these goals. Life is short; make sure you do the most important thing.

3. Don't postpone

The longer you wait to do something, the harder it is to accomplish the task. If you want to reduce stress and demands in your life, plan to act as soon as possible. Making an effort to get the job done as quickly as possible will reduce your burden in the future.

4. Give everything a place

If there is no house, it is easy to get lost. Keeping things organized means keeping your belongings in place. Organized people maintain order by storing things correctly and labelling storage spaces. Provide easy-to-use storage space for what you've been using, and don't let your storage space get messy. Be creative in meeting your storage needs.

As an experiment, choose one place in the house that you can re-organize. If there are dispersed items, then group them together. Once everything is sorted out, identify a suitable "place" for similar items, and label the "homes".

For example, a cup holder for your pens and pencils should go in an easily accessible place, but the rarely used craft materials can be stored out of sight.

5. Declutter daily

Find time each week to reorganize. Highly organized people make sure they set aside a regular time to put things tidy up. Things do not stay organized. The ongoing reorganization is required to stay on track.

6. Keep only what is essential

More stuff means more chaos. People living an orderly life will only keep what meets their needs and what they want. Having fewer things also means you like them more and you feel better when you use all you own, rather than keeping many things and not using any of these things.

Have you ever felt you have no place to keep all your stuff? Get rid of something instead of renting storage units or buying a bigger house. As an experiment, write down the number of things you actually need. Then, list all your assets. If the number of items you own exceeds your ideal demand list, then it's time to sort them out.

7. Know where to dispose of items

Do everything possible to get rid of things. Less stuff means less confusion. Donate to Fair cushion shop. Sell on Craigslist or eBay. Visit the recycling center. Establish garage sales. Find a place to get rid of your stuff.

As an experiment, choose a place in the house to purify. Browse shelves, drawers, and boxes. Set aside everything you don't need. Choose the bunch of things you might want to keep, you can check them later, and now you have to throw a bunch of stuff. Find a way to kick those things out the door right away.

8. Stay away from bargains

You've removed something you don't need. When you see special offers, will you replace them? Instead of bargain shopping without pre-planning, it's better to write down your needs and only buy those items. Organized people will not give in to false advertising. Items on sale only create more chaos.

9. Delegate responsibilities

A truly organized life will not be full of duties, meetings, and deadlines. In fact, it's less full because the poignant things are organized slowly. As an experiment, check your to-do list or create one. Browse the list to find a task that can be deleted from the list or given to others. Now, the pressure to feel the need to do that task has disappeared.10. Work hard

Put in effort. In fact, a lot of effort is often required. After delegating responsibilities and setting a timetable, you can organize what you have to do and when you can do it. Reaching goals requires you to work hard; and realize that when you work harder, you can enjoy tidy family life in the future. When you want to quit today, redouble your efforts.

CHAPTER 20:

Be ready to face business challenges

IT IS UNAVOIDABLE that businesses will face challenges at multiple stages of their growth and expansion. Problems exist to be resolved, and the perfect way to overcome the challenges your business will face is to anticipate these problems and get ready to solve them as they arise. But how do you resolve problems you don't even recognize? This is why you need to understand probable challenges that could affect your business in the future.

The ambiguity of the future

The success of businesses generally depend on the ability to observe current trends in the market and then make decisions or develop strategies grounded on specific forecasts and calculations.

Sadly, the place we live in today is full of many false indicators, mainly because of global economic struggles, fluctuating market trends, an uncertain environment, the rise of competitors, new marketing techniques, etc.

Dependency on clients

If a single customer accounts for more than half of your income, you are an independent contractor, not a business owner.

Devolving the customer base is vital to growing the business, but this can be difficult, especially when the customer pays well and on time.

Unfortunately, this can cause long-term obstacles because even if you have employees, you may still act as a subcontractor to larger companies. This arrangement allows your clients to avoid the risk of increasing wage obligations in areas where work can be exhausted at any time. All these risks have been transferred from larger companies to you. This arrangement can work if your primary customers have constant needs for your products or services. However, it is usually best to have a diverse customer base to reduce the risks them withdrawing payment or no longer working with you.

Cash flow management

In business, it is necessary to have enough cash to pay the bills, but it is also necessary for everyone. Whether it's your business or your life, cash pressure can break you. To avoid this problem, small business owners must either have sufficient capital or supplementary income to support cash reserves when needed. This is why many small businesses continue working and start a business at the same time. While this distraction can make business development difficult, cash shortages make business development impossible.

Cash management becomes even more critical when cash flows to companies and owners. Although dealing with business accounting and taxation may be within the capabilities of most business owners, it is usually best to use professional assistance. The complexity of the company's ledger is increasing with customers and employees, so getting help with bookkeeping can prevent it from becoming a reason not to expand.

Fatigue

For even the most enthusiastic, long hours, effort, and constant pressure will make them feel miserable. Many business owners, even successful business owners, work longer hours than their employees. In addition, they are concerned that their business will stagnate in their absence, so they avoid spending time off work to recharge.

Fatigue can lead to rash decisions about the business, including the desire to quit the business altogether. In the early (usually) small business development days, it can be a challenge to find a way to keep the business going without overwhelming the owner.

Rules and regulations

Just as technology is constantly changing, regulations in business change from time to time. And, companies have to abide by these ever-changing rules and regulations to avoid fines or penalties for violations. Unfortunately, changing regulations and laws are not always consistent with in purpose. For example, higher costs due to environmental taxes (such as carbon taxes) are detriment all to manufacturing companies that release carbon waste. The solution to this problem is to understand the meaning and different types of industry-specific regulations, the impact of these regulations on your business, and develop skills or hire experts or consultants from the tax and health departments to respond to these changing regulations.

Finance and business resource management

Many business owners are people who have dreams or ideas. They are good at spotting market gaps, looking at large pictures, and reconstructive thinking.

Businesses that generate a lot of revenue may seem healthy, but they may actually be dying because spending accounts for a massive share of profits. In this case, any business is highly prone to bankruptcy or default because they have very few reserves. Unexpected increases in costs or spending or recessionary winds can easily blow this business down, which is why business owners need to manage their finances and resources carefully themselves or with the help of experts.

Technology advancement and changes

Sometimes different technologies are developed to make business operations and activities faster and more efficient. Keeping up with these technological advances can be a challenging task. Ultimately, customers will leave businesses not operating or following the trend of technological progress.

Therefore, depending on its size, an enterprise will have to deploy the right technical solutions and automation for its business operations, financial and resource management, and performance tracking. On the other hand, they must also choose the right technology carefully for their size and capital, so as not to spend too much with little ROI.

Hiring the right people for the job

Hiring and employing new employees can be a tough task. You have to hire the right people with the right skills, interests and determination to help your business develop. Hiring also depends on the size of your business, which means that when hiring, you have to consider the type of employees your business needs, whether part-time or full-time.

Many skills can be required to operate and grow your business such as such as IT, hard and soft and transferable skills (such as foreign languages) and problem-solving skills). For example, essay writing companies like Assign Geek have excellent customer service and coordinating roles, as well as selecting employees with excellent writing and research skills and a perfect academic background to support their essay and essay writing services.

Marketing and client relationship management

We live in a digital age. Customers can access a lot of information and rely heavily on peer recommendations. Therefore, unlike the traditional marketing era, companies and enterprises establish contact with customers in new ways. Now companies have to become more customer-centric in almost every aspect of business (like marketing, product design, and development) to acquire and retain customers.

Therefore, all business owners must find the right channels to communicate with potential customers and increase brand awareness. To properly manage customer relationships, companies must also provide social media accounts, websites, chat options, toll-free calls, email, and other options so customers can make complaints and provide feedback.

Observing performance and key performance indicators

Any business that cannot monitor its performance and key performance indicators is doomed to failure. Therefore, companies must determine the right key performance indicators that need to be monitored. Enterprises must analyze their KPIs and communicate the results and analysis to employees to improve employee cohesion and to enable employees to help achieve business goals and improve decision-making.

Striking a balance between quality and growth

Even when companies do not rely on founders, the problems caused by growth sometimes seem to solve or even outweigh their benefits. Whether it's a service or a product, companies must sacrifice to scale. This can mean you no longer can personally manage every customer relationship or check every gadget.

Unfortunately, it is usually only personal involvement and attention to detail that can make a business successful. As a result, many small business owners are often bound by holding too tightly, harming the company's growth. There is a big gap between shoddy work and an unhealthy obsession with quality. Business owners should develop the company's processes to find a solution to scale and grow without damaging the brand.

In conclusion, every business faces numerous challenges.

However, if you can anticipate the challenges listed above, when they do appear, you would be better able to deal with them.

To order more copies of this book, find books by other Canadian authors, or make inquiries about publishing your own book, contact PageMaster at:

PageMaster Publication Services Inc. 11340-120 Street, Edmonton, AB T5G 0W5
books@pagemaster.ca
780-425-9303

catalogue and e-commerce store **PageMasterPublishing.ca**

About the Author

KIDANE ARAYA WAS born in Adi-mekeda, Eritrea in 1972. He grew up on a farm and despite experiencing its benefits he knew that being a businessman was in his future. In the late nineties, Kidane opened a textile firm in Adi-mekeda but later decided he wanted a more wholesome life for his family. He moved to Germany to further his studies and eventually brought his family there as well. In 2013 Kidane and his family became Canadian citizens.

Kidane attributes his progress and the actualization of his dream to settle in Canada to the inspiration and stalwart support of his wife, Tsege Ghebretinsae.

In 2007, Kidane opened All Canada Clean Corp. and it has flourished into a thriving business today. He has also started many businesses in Ethiopia, Uganda, Dubai, China and Europe.

Kidane has learned life-fulfilling lessons by through business. He now wishes to pass on his life-long learnings, about how starting a business is a viable venture and well worth the efforts. But more importantly, he wants to emphasize the keys to achieving success which are applying faith to daily life, staying inspired yourself, and having a supportive family.

www.ingramcontent.com/pod-product-compliance
Lightning Source LLC
LaVergne TN
LVHW021524080426
835509LV00018B/2650